GAIN THE POWER OF POSITIVE THOUGHT

The Key to Success

GW00702144

GAIN THE POWER OF POSITIVE THOUGHT

The Key to Success

Gilbert Oakley

foulsham

LONDON • NEW YORK • TORONTO • SYDNEY

foulsham

The Publishing House, Bennetts Close,
Cippenham, Berkshire SL1 5AP.

ISBN 0-572-02336-7
Copyright © 1989 and 1997 W. Foulsham and Co. Ltd

Typeset in Great Britain by
Rowland Phototypesetting Limited,
Bury St Edmunds, Suffolk.
Printed by St Edmundsbury Press Limited,
Bury St Edmunds, Suffolk.

CONTENTS

INTRODUCTION

In the years between the two world wars a quite popular mental and emotional condition afflicted many men, women and teenagers too. It was considerably useful as an excuse for not getting on in life and for being a failure in many things.

This mental malady was referred to as an inferiority complex. Many concerns sprang up during those years to help to combat this emotional affliction by home study courses and correspondence courses, among which was the Institute of Pelmanism, whose chief consultant and analyst was my father, T. Gilbert Oakley. In addition, there is the British Institute of Practical Psychology, another praiseworthy concern whose aim it is to cure people of the much-dreaded inferiority complex and to assist those who feel they suffer from inferior feelings.

Today, however, an inferiority complex is heard of less frequently and, in the shining light of present progress, there is little room for feeling inferior. Nevertheless there still exists a negative approach to life suffered by thousands of people all over this computerised, Filofaxed, personally organised, nuclear-conscious, space-aged world.

This is best described as an inadequacy complex. It can be just as damning as the original inferiority complex.

There is a new generation of success-craving, sophisticated, fashion- and work-conscious men and women of all ages, who want their own Mercs, Porsches, their own flats and penthouses or town and country homes. They want highly-paid careers, not just jobs, with good prospects and promotion.

They are not overly enthusiastic about live-in loving. Life in squats and the communes of ten or 20 years ago hold little interest for them. Pop music, compact discs, tapes, telly and discos are their main relaxations from hard, profitable money-and-success-making sessions.

Personal style and image are important and they all aim to be adequate. They are today's high achievers. Today's fast-talking, street-wise young men and women. Those between 21 and 30 are earning far more than their parents ever dreamed of at a similar age. Most young people have a bank account, many invest in stocks and shares and it is unthinkable for them to be without a credit card. The menace of AIDS has replaced one-night stands with basic, steady emotional relationships.

In direct opposition to this section of the population are the unemployed. They are the victims of this generation. Often they are unemployed only because of where they were born, sometimes coupled with a bad home environment, bad education or bad parenting. High unemployment has made people more conscious of the need to get a good education and qualifications. The sixties, a time of relative high employment, was also a time of protest. Nearly every university campus was seething with unrest. Times have changed and now if you do not make the grade you can feel inadequate and, in fact, are often made to feel so by your peers.

Others feel inadequate because they just cannot get employment that suits their particular abilities, or cannot get jobs that can make use of their special talents.

There are a few in every society who are shiftless and who do not want to work. Provided they have enough for their immediate physical needs – food, drink, cigarettes – the future holds no fears for them. But more people are recognising that if they want the comforts and luxuries of life they must work for them. It is only when they cannot achieve this ambition that they feel inadequate and frustrated and then it is all too easy to give up. But if they have the desire to struggle on then this book will help them to develop the habit of positive thinking that will help them win through. We cannot all be millionaires but even if your life falls somewhat short of your expectations it can still be a full and a colourful existence. It is a cliché to say that money isn't everything, but thinking positively is not just a means to fulfilling ambitions. It is also the key that will open other doors, maybe in the way of satisfying hobbies or even alternative means of earning a more interesting living.

This book is aimed at those who want to improve their lot in life, who maybe recognise that they do not always see things in the most positive manner but who have a genuine willingness to improve their outlook. As with a computer, we must feed the correct information into our brain to get the result we desire.

Positive-minded people do not feed incorrect data into their brains, neither do they press the wrong key and get a negative print-out. It is with those people we will be dealing in this book. And also with those who do, from time to time, give themselves negative information based on past unfortunate experiences and who, as a result, develop into negative human beings instead of positive people.

Adequate, positive people, male or female, indulge in enterprise, have powers of endurance, are achievers. They specialise rather than generalise. They have positive convictions and are not defeatist. They indulge freely in positive self-expression to bring out personality. They don't refute the power of faith in their most troublesome moments. They can be cool and laid-back in a crisis. They readily apply the human touch in a commercialised and a computerised world when necessary.

In effect, they are adequate enough to face up to every situation in their domestic, social and commercial life because they are positive they are *right*. And right is might – there can be no doubt about it!

Gilbert Oakley
London 1989

1

NEGATIVE THOUGHTS FROM THE PAST

You know your past is behind you but your present can be negatively influenced by dwelling upon what has happened in a string of 'yesterdays'. Thousands of negative-minded people live in the past, in the shadows of what went wrong, what mistakes were made and what opportunities were lost. They constantly recall friends who were disillusioned, loved ones who are gone.

Happily, things are not always the same a second time round. That goes for success as well as for failure, of course. But success we can control to a very large degree, whereas failure has a nasty way of dogging us if we are not very careful. Mental attitude towards past failures in life can either minimize them or exaggerate their importance with consequent positive or negative effects upon the vital question of *today*.

Those who live in the past while struggling with the present, with a shaky and a doubtful eye upon the immediate future, develop a complex. While we have suggested that inferiority is a thing of the past, a complex is still a very *real* thing, a condition that any sort of progress will fail to dismiss until strong efforts are made to fight it.

A complex is a number of repressed and consciously forgotten, but subconsciously retained, ideas, memories and impressions to which are ascribed abnormal mental conditions and, very often, abnormal physical conditions. All are due to mental and emotional attitudes and reactions that affect the conscious mind but cannot be lifted up out of the subconscious and recognised for what they are. The analyst in the psychiatrist's consulting room can release these hidden repressed negative memories and impressions. But this is a slow process which can be expensive.

Far better to be your own analyst and psychiatrist. As long as you are prepared to be honest with yourself this will be possible. Some deep-rooted problems do need a psychiatrist to bring them to the surface, but if you are trying to make yourself into a more positive person you can indulge in a little private self-analysis.

Feelings of inadequacy arise from deep-seated convictions that the decisions you make are the wrong ones and you will be incapable of dealing with certain situations because, in the past, similar circumstances and conditions resulted in failure on your part. So, of course, it will happen again. And you will make it happen again by fearing that the past *will* repeat itself. Therefore you dare not trust your convictions today because of what happened yesterday. Maybe you acted upon well-meant but incorrect advice which you had received in good faith. You should accept that things need never be the same twice.

Someone put negative ideas into your mind in the past and you have lived with them ever since. You have fostered these ideas for so long now that they have become part of your lifestyle. You have forgotten who said what and where, but you do remember it *was* said sometime, somewhere. So influenced, you react today as if it had just happened and the result is you fail again. You feel and become inadequate.

Maybe you are afraid to face up to life and find it far easier to give up the fight and to accept defeat before you have made any attack at all. In that state of negative mindedness no one is likely to offer you any sort of responsibility and you will remain just where you are, discounted and dismissed as being of no account.

Are you inadequate but don't wish to be, or are you inadequate because you secretly want to be, because it is the easier way out?

We are accepting that you do not want to be inadequate. That you are interested in the amazing influence of positive thought and its great powers to overcome negativity. You want to forge ahead whether you are young or pushing on a bit, for at 40 there is still almost half a lifetime ahead of you and at 20 the world is at your feet.

In that frame of mind, and remembering that the past influences the present and can well decide the future, we will delve a little bit into your succession of 'yesterdays'.

1 Were you happy with your parents?

If not, does it really matter now? Do you still live in the shadow of your parents' dictates of a negative, repressive nature? Parenthood is

11

a primitive state anyway. Fathers may be jealous of sons in case they do better than themselves. They may be over-protective or even, occasionally, secretly, but passively, sexually attracted to their daughters and try to prevent them associating with boys and young men. This gives rise to jealousy on the part of the father. Mothers may be jealous of their daughters growing pretty and looking as they did in former years and may try to deny them the companionship of young men. Mothers may yearn to keep their sons for ever young, trying to deny them the loving companionship of other females. Mothers may fear the thought of their daughters becoming career women and making more money and achieving more success than they did when they were working girls.

There may be jealousy and antagonism between siblings. Favourite sons and daughters may make less favoured brothers and sisters feel unwanted and inadequate.

From those emotional attitudes on the part of parents, sons and daughters can be made to feel unwanted, unloved, useless and inadequately equipped to face up to life outside the family circle.

Think back on your childhood. Was it affected by circumstances similar to those described above?

2 Did you make friends easily at school and after school?

Friendships formed in schooldays are frequently erratic and often unstable. There comes the difficult age when boys and girls pass from asexuality, when they have no sexual inclinations, to bi-sexuality, which can involve erotic attitudes towards both boys and girls. From this they pass through to the homosexual and lesbian stage when schoolboy and schoolgirl 'crushes' are developed towards male and female teachers or towards other members of their own sex. Passing normally and happily through those stages of emotional development, there comes the heterosexual stage, when boys and girls recognise and accept each other as their natural partners in life.

After those vital and perfectly natural and acceptable stages in adolescent development are overcome, friendships are formed that are devoid of sexual overtones and the meaning of genuine friendship becomes apparent and acceptable.

There are, of course, those who do not pass through the bisexual or homosexual stages. They are the ones who accept and develop lesbian and homosexual attitudes and emotions which, today, in a more enlightened society, are not condemned as they were in the days of, say, Oscar Wilde.

Emotional traumas in adolescence often leave their mark on the young male and female adult and some people are affected by first sexual contacts all their lives. For the majority, though, the sexual vagaries of schooldays are quickly forgotten; friends are made easily and friendships deepen as the years go by.

What was your adolescence like?

3 Did teachers make you feel a fool in school and at games?

More teachers are responsible for making a boy or girl feel inadequate in later life than would be imagined. Although the inculcating of the three Rs has radically changed since the Second World War, pupils are still open to ridicule and insults levelled at them by their teachers. The student who is slow to learn or not bright academically is often made to feel inadequate before an entire class just as his predecessor was in the more authoritarian schools of yesterday.

Games teaches can still make the uncompetitive schoolboy or schoolgirl, with no penchant for kicking a football round a pitch or throwing a ball into a basket or scoring runs at cricket, feel an absolute fool on the games field in front of the rest of the class. Many a battle may have been won on the playing fields of Eton and Harrow in the past, but many children's hopes in the battlefield of life have been lost in squalid playgrounds and football pitches of today's educational establishments.

Many an adult, male or female, could trace back feelings of negativism and inadequacy to treatment received at the hands of insensitive schoolteachers.

Do you have happy memories of your schooldays, or not?

4 Did something negative happen in your first job?

In these days of high unemployment, the first kind of work experience that a school-leaver has is often a youth training scheme. These vary in quality and usefulness, depending on the employer. It should be an introduction to being in a work situation coupled with on-the-spot training. Unfortunately, some employers see their young workers as a source of cheap labour and teenagers who are keen to learn can find it a frustrating experience to discover that only menial work is expected of them.

Even if the first job does come up to expectations, often mistakes are made through unfamiliarity with the routine that bring a blush to the cheeks whenever the occasion is remembered. What the young worker must not do is let an incident like this blight the path to what could be a bright future.

Think back to your first job – was it a pleasant experience, or not?

5 The first time you fell in love – was it good or bad?

Your very first adult feelings for the opposite sex in a relationship are very often embarrassing, compulsive, bewildering and a strange mixture of sexual desire and genuine fondness and love. Quite often it is difficult to decide which is the stronger impulse – sexual desire or genuine love. Young males are apt to mistake physical feelings for love whereas young females prefer to accept love as the dominating factor that leads, in a natural way, to sexual expression. If the female suspects real love is absent or is thinly disguised in terms of sexual expression, she is likely to hesitate. The male, on the other hand, with his wish to appear macho and masculine may well think his sexual overtures and evidence of his prowess are sufficiently symbolic of true love to influence the female into compliance. That, of course, is OK for chance encounters, one-night stands and short, casual relationships, but it doesn't bode well for a stable long-term involvement. Now, with the ever-present threat of AIDS, men and women of all ages are more cautious in their relationships with each other. Nevertheless, emotional mistakes and errors of judgement can still be made and a promising love affair can go by the board through lack of feeling and consideration and by not making due allowances for each other.

Today's trend for live-in lovers has a lot going for it. When marriage is not the binding factor there has to be a commitment on both sides to make the relationship work. But even with a determination to succeed things do not always work out and it is better to discover that you are not compatible before rather than after marriage. Even though breaking up is a harrowing experience in any circumstance, if you have not taken the plunge into married life then there is not the trauma of a divorce to go through.

Jealousy can arise both in and out of marriage and it is a very destructive emotion. Relationships have to be very secure to combat the strength of feeling involved when one person in a relationship thinks, rightly or wrongly, that his or her partner is being unfaithful. Closely linked with jealousy is possessiveness, when one half of a relationship cannot bear to think of the other half in company with a member of the opposite sex.

Often these feelings are not based on fact, but rather on suspicion. However, whether there is a genuine basis for these suspicions or not, a feeling of inadequacy is present because the 'wronged' partner feels he or she is deficient somehow, whereas the rival has that 'certain something' that is causing the attraction.

Actual feelings, imagined or otherwise, of sexual inadequacy and extremes of over-possessiveness are age-old destroyers of the emotion of love. Mistrust and suspicion, doubt and denial follow in quick succession and a love-partnership can dissolve in acrimony, casting negative shadows over any future emotional alliance with a new partner. First love affairs can very often be the killing-fields for future more adult relationships if the emotional and physical mistakes of the past are permitted to invade the present.

Can you look back on your first love-relationships with happy memories, or were they so disastrous that they have blighted future friendships?

Now sum up

Think of all the possible negative things of the past that may, today, be making you feel inadequate. As you reflect, you may see how these former experiences are shaping your outlook and robbing you of the power to apply positive thought to present situations that could make your day and mould your future.

1 *You may not have been happy with your parents, or your brothers and sisters.*

2 *You may have been harassed at school and unable to make friends easily.*

3 *You may have been made to feel a fool by teachers at school.*

4 *You may have had unfortunate experiences in your first job.*

5 *Your first love-relationships may have gone wrong.*

Those five initial experiences involved what you thought about yourself engendered by what others thought about you and said to you.

Those negative thoughts within yourself and about yourself, created by people in your past, now influence your present and could ruin your future – unless you use the amazing influence of positive thought from now on.

2

POSITIVE THOUGHTS FOR
THE PRESENT

Do you know what you want out of life? Are you ambitious or content to be blown by the wind? If you are mediocre at lots of things, try to become proficient in one particular thing. Many children who are not academically gifted suddenly find, in their teens, that they have an aptitude for a particular sport or pastime that requires manual dexterity and they become the envy of their friends.

If we have the patience and persistence we can all discover where our particular skill lies. We now have so many choices as society is far less rigid than it was a few years ago. We can choose to marry or not; we can decide whether to start a family or not; and if or when babies do come along we can decide who should stay at home and look after them. Although some jobs that, on the whole, attract women are still very badly paid, there are many occupations where women can earn the same as men, so a couple can choose whether father or mother will look after the children while they are of pre-school age. Having made a positive choice to be the 'househusband' a man is often more content to stay at home than a woman might be. She may begrudge the fact that she is expected to give up work just because she is a woman, thus putting her career prospects back a few years.

Women can compete with men on an equal footing in almost every walk of life now (the Church, however, generally being a notable exception) and are forced to make positive choices as to which way their career and personal life should go.

In the past, women were ambitious for:

a man with a good earning capacity;

a home with things in it better than their neighbour's;

children;

a contented home life;

grandchildren.

And the most men wanted from life was:

a woman who could be mother, sister, wife, mistress;

a neat home;

enough money to provide a decent standard of living;

men friends to drink with;

a son, but a daughter would do.

There are still some people who cling to the role models of yesterday because that gives them a feeling of security. They recognise the role that society has ordained for them and are happy to fill it. No choice, no responsibility is required. But, all the same, they come to feel left behind as they see friends and relations fitting into the new open society that offers greater freedoms.

Easily obtainable ambitions can make for contentment in life. But contentment can often become disastrously boring. Then dawns that niggling, irritating conviction that there should be more to life than convention, more to existence than that followed slavishly by the Smiths and the Joneses and the Browns in their bland, surburban contentedness. That is the time when certain little brain cells start to alert the individual to the fact they are not being used. Hidden talents have been by-passed by the safe pursuit of convention and by sticking with the safe past rather than plunging into an unknown future.

That is positive thought attempting to break through. There is something missing.

This is illustrated so many times in the media when quite ordinary people suddenly determine to break the bonds of convention and strike out for something new – something they know full well they can do but have discarded, possibly because of past discouragements or lack of the will to win.

These are men and women who have seen something they want, and have worked flat out to get it.

The young have a clear path where choices and ambitions are

concerned; those with families and responsibilities have a harder time. They must decide if they are really serious in their attempt to change course, or if it is a passing whim because that particular day has gone badly.

A hidden, unrealised talent must be explored and exploited if repression and frustration are not to set in.

Let us examine some hidden talents that positive thinking could bring to the surface, thus changing the old way of life for ever:

an ability to sing (pop or classical);

an ability to act (comedy or drama);

an ability to draw, paint, design, sculpt;

an ability to write books, novels, plays;

an ability to play a musical instrument;

an ability to be a computer operator, a financial wizard;

an ability to be a visualiser, copy-writer in an advertising agency;

an ability or desire to study for a degree;

an ability to sell or market merchandise;

an ability to handle estate agency work;

an ability to handle accountancy;

an ability to be in catering;

an ability to be a video director;

an ability to be a PR executive;

an ability to be on the Stock Exchange;

an ability to be in electronics;

an ability to be in television and film production or theatre production.

Today the list is almost endless. The potential is there in every single, normal brain to handle successfully at least one of the special abilities just outlined.

What is so brilliantly new is the suddenly-realised power of positive thought that, properly applied, can raise the hitherto conventional man or woman of almost any age from the mundane existence of conventionality to that of supreme individuality.

Think of the woman who started to design clothes in the drawing room of her home and who now runs a chain of shops selling her designer clothes.

Think of the man who first fiddled with a small television set and later developed that marvellous electronic device called a computer.

Think of the man who could not write a note of music but whose songs have been played round the world now for decades.

Think of . . . well, there is no end to the ideas, inventions, discoveries, medical cures, methods of home entertainment, domestic appliances and so on that have been promoted over the decades simply by the amazing influence of positive thinking; by the discovery and nurturing of a particular talent that has lain dormant for years until the suddent inspiration of imagination and determination has exploded into actual fact.

You, now, pondering over this undeniable truism, possibly after having felt for a long time that there *is* something productive or creative that you can do, what are you gong to do about it?

This is what you are going to do

1 Examine all the fields into which your special abilities will fit.

2 Choose one particular sphere and line of thought you feel applies.

3 Develop your particular capability to its fullest extent.

4 Get to know people who specialise in your chosen sphere.

5 Visualise yourself as being one of them.

6 Sell yourself to them by projecting positive thoughts to them.

7 Develop your own business along similar lines.

Positive thinking now will decide your prospects for the future. It may well help you to rise to an executive position. Or positive thought could inspire you to go it alone.

Whichever course you choose the maxim is: 'I *can* do it and I *will* do it'.

So, what sort of a person are you, positive or negative, one of the herd or an individual in your own right? Let us examine that question in the following chapter.

3

ARE YOU AN 'I AM'?

The progressive people mentioned in the last chapter who started out on their own and made it to the big time were 'I am' people. They visualised and then they realised. For many hundreds of years, people believed that the mind and the body were separate, that the mind had no control over the body. Now, of course, we know differently. Doctors and those who specialise in the study of the mind recognise and accept the very obvious body/mind relationship. A relationship that can cause the depressed and oppressed mind to bring about functional illnesses in the body and, in reverse, can cause the happy progressive, ambitious mind to enervate and rejuvenate the body to the extent that many things become possible in the face of opposition and competition.

Being an 'I am' person promotes good health which, in turn, causes thought power to be highly charged and dynamic. The 'I am' syndrome defeats inadequacy and feelings of failure.

But do not confuse the 'I am' personality with the egotist who overrates his or her abilities and talents, talks big but thinks small, and puts himself or herself first to the total exclusion of others.

On the other hand, the 'I am' person is an individual who recognises the scope of particular talents and abilities while acknowledging their limitations. This person does not attempt to live above their mental income and therefore does not run into emotional debt.

It is good for people to look at an 'I am' personality and to say, without reserve, 'Yes, you *are*'!

The 'I am nots' get up each morning, travel on crowded buses, trains and the underground, or sit in their cars in endless traffic jams. They arrive at their place of work and, for hours on end, day in, day out, week in, week out, put a screw into a hole, connect this wire to that wire, paint this red and that black, add up figures, tap keys on the computer, answer the phone, put cards into files, type letters, hammer this in, force that out, open one door, close another. At the end of it all, they arrive home exhausted after the invariable sardine-like journey.

Good, of course, in these days of unemployment. Regular jobs, regular money. Not to be laughed at. Some people enjoy the security of routine. But, in those crowded buses and trains and streets and offices and factories and shops and stores and super-markets are 'I am' people struggling to get out of the rut and to amount to something which is, for them, better. Some escape, others never do.

Those who do manage to break through become leaders, instead of the led. Or they decide to break out on their own and become their own driving force rather than being merely cogs in other people's wheels.

Being an 'I am' is something of a job. It is, in fact, a highly specialised occupation. When you are first born you *are* an individual. Attention is lavished on you. You are an 'I am' in no uncertain manner. Then parents take you in hand and attempt to mould you into their conceptions of how they want their offspring to be. After that, it is the turn of teachers and educationalists in various spheres of youthful upbringing. We are not always lucky enough to have special talents recognised and nurtured and developed. They may go against the parental grain. Teaching authorities may not take account of them in their school curriculum. So, many are prepared to be just one of the crowd. Far more comfortable for parents to have their son in a 'safe job', for daughters to become eventual mothers and bear children so that mothers and fathers can relive their days all over again, but this time as doting grandparents. But we have noted, have we not, that this is the age of the on-going success-individual? – the street-wise youngster eager to get the very best out of life, to earn good 'bread', to be one of the 'I ams' rather than one of the 'I wish I could bes'?

The magnetism of desire becomes an ever-present compulsion in the minds of those young enough still to have ambitions. Furious hoping and thinking and planning gradually develop into firm convictions that the power of this concentrated thought can and will bring the desired goals.

How simple it all seems, you may well say.

So, I will digress for a few paragraphs in order to show how really very simple *is* the application of the power of positive thinking. Bear in mind that the events to be related took place in the thirties, the forties and the fifties, eras when the degrees of progress had not advanced so much as they did in the eighties and continue to do in the nineties.

1 As a boy of seven I decided I wanted to be a writer. After many unsuccessful efforts I at last got a short story published in a magazine. During the remaining years of my schooling I won several prizes for essays and compositions. All the time my mind was concentrated on the dominant belief that I would, one day, be a professional writer. Throughout my teens until I was called up for the Second World War I wrote plays and short stories but did not submit any of them for I was not sure I had reached the degree of competence I hoped for. Throughout the war, whenever it was possible, I continued to write. The power of the thought of me as a writer persisted. After the war I continued and, in 1954, I had my first book published. I had decided to specialise in practical books rather than in fiction. Up to date (1997) I have written and had published over 200 books.

Facts established:

I had recognised a talent. The power of thought had enabled me to project it to others and I became a writer.

2 In addition to my desire, at the age of seven, to become a writer, I also wished to be able to play the piano in an accomplished manner, but I did not want to go through the trials and the troubles of learning how to read music. I started to finger the keyboard and longed for the day when I could stretch over an octave with each hand. When finally I could, I discovered the joy of playing major and minor keys, playing in the bass with the left hand while doing something quite different in the treble, but in harmony with the bass. Then came the pleasure of improvisation and composition as well as learning how to play popular music and the classics in my own chords and with my own arrangements. During the war I played often in ENSA concerts and, after the war, in clubs and at social events.

Facts established:

I had recognised a talent. The power of thought had given me the confidence to project it to others and I became a pianist.

3 After the war, and in between writing books, I became interested in commercial art and graphics. For a solid year I concentrated on developing styles of hand-painted lettering and design. For many years after that I sold graphic designs and posters and window displays all over London.

Facts established:

I had recognised a talent. The power of thought had helped me develop that talent, others recognised it and I became a graphic artist.

4 In the late fifties I was offered the editorship of what was to be a national health magazine. With no knowledge of editorship or magazine layout I took the post and my concentrated thought power produced the confidence to persuade me that I could be a successful editor. My graphics experience helped me design layouts and my literary experience helped me edit other authors' work.

Facts established:

I had recognised how two talents could be merged successfully. The power of thought told me it could be so, and it was.

The world is full of things that *can* be done and *have* been done. There are people who can do them. The late Liberace could not read music, yet he *thought* he could entertain at the keyboard and his power of thought helped him to do so. Irving Berlin could not write scores for the keyboard yet his songs are still being sung all over the world. The late artist, Lowry, *thought* he couldn't paint. Sadly, his lack of positive thought resulted in him becoming famous only after his death. Beethoven, after deafness afflicted him, still desperately wanted to compose. He could no longer hear the notes on the piano so he *thought* them instead and went on to compose more wonderful music. Sir Richard Attenborough acted in indifferent films as a youth, yet *thought* he could become a film director. Today his power of thought has raised him to the ranks of a major British film director. A certain lady, daughter of a grocer in a corner shop in Grantham, *thought* she could become Prime Minister. She did. Toulouse-Lautrec, with his terrible affliction of being a lame dwarf, *thought* he could paint. He could and he did and his name is still a household word the world over. Logie Baird *thought* he could make living people appear, in movement, on a tiny screen. He did and today we have television. Marconi *thought* about wireless and it happened.

All those celebrities, and thousands more like them, sung and unsung, are the results of 'I *want* to be and therefore I *am*' thinking.

The question of jobs and careers is very often determined by your attitude towards yourself: whether, in fact, you are a positive thinker or not. So let us now examine that.

4

THE CAREER SYNDROME

There are five different states of mind and material conditions and circumstances relative to the work or career syndrome.

1 *Starting your job*

2 *Wanting a change of job*

3 *Gaining promotion*

4 *Losing your job*

5 *Not having a job*

Each condition and circumstance involves a state of mind that should be positive if success is to be achieved, even in the unhappy circumstances of not having a job. With the word 'job' we must involve the word career, for a job can be merely a passing period of time whereas a career can involve a lifetime of gainful employment with a pleasant pensioned retirement when the time arrives.

Many people drift from job to job, each job involving a different kind of work. The drifter seldom markets any specific ability. Indeed, he or she probably never considers the possibility that they may, in fact, possess a certain ability that could, if recognised, carve out a lasting career rather than merely provide a succession of passing periods of work. In Chapter Two we examined a host of possible personal abilities that could be recognised and utilised in order to shape and form a consistent career. In this chapter we are going to assume that a specific ability has been recognised and that a strong desire to cash in on that particular ability has been created in the individual. We will leave age out of it, as many promising and fulfilling careers have been started by men and women of any age from 20 to 50, in spite of the employment difficulties that exist today.

1 Starting your job

If the job involves the utilisation of a particular ability you have recognised and have determined to cultivate, look upon this first job as a positive step towards the development of your particular talent and not merely as a source of income until something better turns up. This will be accomplished by learning all you can from your workmates and your employers, from the very first rung on the ladder. Project a positive and keen interest in all that the work involves. Ask leading questions and make notes of the answers. Be positive, also, in making suggestions for possible improvements. Wait a few weeks before you do this, though, as no one likes the know-all who has only been in the job five minutes and promptly tells the other workers how the firm should be run! Your positive personality, without being overbearing, will make a good impression on your immediate superiors and, of course, on your boss. Accept in good grace mistakes you may initially make and act upon all advice given to you. Watch your immediate superiors closely, gauging just how they gained the positions they have over the rest of the staff for, one day, you will want promotion yourself. Never show any element of 'big-headedness', but in a cool, calm and positive manner be just that little way ahead of the others so that, eventually, they come to *you* for advice and suggestions. Remember that career-building is a matter of years, not weeks or months, so do not be impatient. Your powers of positive thought will tell in the long run, for it will be quite possible that you will be working with others who may well be content to stay as they are, toiling away mechanically day after day, with no really positive desire towards building a more rosy future for themselves. But you will be different.

2 Wanting a change of job

Perhaps, in your present job, you are convinced your special talents and abilities are not being utilised to their fullest. You feel frustrated, longing to break free and explore other fields in your specialised work. Working to live is one thing. It can be mundane and boring. Living to work is quite another thing. It is vital and fulfilling. So, if your present job seems to be merely a way of making money in order to live, and your talents and abilities are not being used to the full, the answer is to get out and to start afresh. The positive attitude to work and career is to love it; to wake up each morning raring to get to your place of work; maybe to be just that little bit reluctant to leave it in the evening. But there is always tomorrow which, after an evening's relaxation and a good night's sleep, can be attacked again with even more enthusiasm.

And that, surely, is the attitude of the positive thinker. If you do not have that positive attitude towards the use of your talents and abilities you just must get out of it and into something better, probably in the same field of activity, that exploits to the full just what you know you can do best. We must sensibly agree that security *is* a good thing, a decent salary *is* much to be desired. But if a job is frustrating and soul-destroying then much harm is done to the mind and, subsequently, to the body. The personality becomes negative and a sense of inadequacy begins to creep in.

Reading this, many of you living in areas of high unemployment will say, 'It's all very well talking like that but what if there are no jobs at all to go to, let alone having several jobs to choose from?'

We must concede that in these instances positive thinking may have to be directed elsewhere. If you cannot move from an area because of family ties or cost of housing, then life is made very difficult. Even so, spend some time either thinking alone or talking over possibilities with family and friends. What are your areas of interest? Have you any hobbies? Could you possibly turn a hobby, such as carpentry, into a part-time activity with the hope of becoming fully self-employed at some time in the future? If you feel your skills and abilities are not good enough, could you join an evening class to brush up your techniques? Maybe you could sell wooden toys to craft centres or local shops to start you off.

There are many people who have turned hobbies into money-making ventures or, having identified a gap in the market, have filled it. With so many households where both the husband and wife work there is a need for someone to come in once or twice a week to do the cleaning. If you enjoy housework or are super-efficient at it, why not start up your own cleaning business? You will probably be surprised at the response you get.

Other services that a working couple would pay to have done for them might involve window cleaning, decorating, party or dinner party catering, the weekly shopping, gardening, ironing, house repairs and so on. If you are unemployed why not give it a try, or if you are in a dead-end job, test the market by advertising to do jobs at weekends before you throw up a secure job to go it alone.

If you do your planning and budgeting well, you might even persuade your bank to give you a loan to start your own business, or you could get help or advice from a government scheme. Success has been achieved in this way in many different fields including fashion, design, photography, publishing, textiles, electronics, computers and many more.

The United Kingdom is full of people who have 'gone it alone' and who have succeeded beyond their wildest dreams, whose companies and concerns have become household names. And that is forgetting the rest of the world and *its* positive thinkers. The motto here is: 'If you cannot join them, beat them!'

3 Gaining promotion

It is said that if you wish to influence someone you should gaze at the spot on the forehead where the pituitary gland is situated. This is at the base of the skull between the eyes. If you try it on your boss when asking for promotion it will seem as though you are looking him or her straight in the eyes. Perhaps this is why it is deemed to work! He or she is impressed by your unblinking gaze and feels you are just the sort of steady, reliable person who should be given promotion.

Rehearse your promotion-seeking speech well. (Try both it and your concentrated gaze out on a friend first to get a reaction.) Give an account of the number of years you have been with the company, the work you have accomplished, possible improvements you may have made in your department, suggestions for future developments. *Will* your thoughts and what you are saying *into* his mind. A clear, decisive voice, good enunciation and conviction will add strength to your pronouncements. Tell your boss what your monthly pay cheque is, why you want to move up in the company and your qualifications for being promoted. This attitude and forthright delivery should impress. He or she will recognise your business-like way of going about it with no dithering or hesitation.

Another excellent approach would be to put it all down in a memo, neatly written or printed out, containing all the information outlined above and asking for a personal interview. When the interview has been granted the facts are already there on your boss's desk, in black and white. You should then repeat them and enlarge upon them so that there is no doubt about your wishes and reasons for wanting promotion. Be as good as your memo appeared to make you. Live up to it. Be frank. Be candid. Be positive. If they wish to delve into your private and/or family affairs, indulge them, for on many of those facts they may well assess the value promotion would have on you, thereby making you happier as a human being as well as more efficient as a worker in the company.

It is unnecessary to add that your personal appearance at the interview should be compatible with the strength of your words, the power of your voice and the courage of your convictions. Let it all follow through as a convincing demonstration of positive thought in action. If this initial attack fails, or is put off for the time being, determine to confront your boss yet again on a future occasion, with a decent and respectful time limit in between the interviews. They will be impressed by your perseverance and one day everything will click and fall into place.

4 Losing your job

There can be a good few reasons for this unfortunate situation over-taking you. You may have lost your job through incompetence, poor knowledge of your work, lack of interest in it, laziness, lack of speed in manual dexterity, lack of an ability to make positive decisions, inability to accept delegation, or to work satisfactorily under your immediate superiors, disagreement with rules and regulations, or absolute boredom with what you consider to be a dead-end occupation. There can also the the winding-up of the firm for whom you are working, and the big bogey of today – redundancy.

Whatever the reason may be for your having to leave your place of employment you simply must not feel you have lost face or become dejected and start to feel inadequate – that old feeling of inferiority. Think very carefully, looking back on the reasons for losing the job. If you lost it because you were not really doing the work best suited to your abilities, capabilities and talents, carry out a searching analysis of yourself and of the things you are best at. This was amply stressed in Chapter Two, when possible alternative abilities were outlined. If the job from which you have now been sacked did not embrace any of your main abilities then, naturally, your daily tasks became dull and routine, uninspiring and ultimately unproductive. But the urgent need to be employed and earning cash and keeping yourself and, possibly, a family as well, thwarted you in the pursuit of your real ambitions and the exploitation of your real abilities.

Many an art school student has abandoned art in the long run because he or she has discovered that acting for the theatre, the screen and television is their real forte. There are probably many industrial or commercial salesmen who have discovered that writing novels or works of a practical nature is the thing they want to do in life. Many a seamstress has turned to dress designing and has eventually carved out a solo career for herself.

Practically everyone is adequate at something that is quite outside the limitations of an everyday, mundane occupation pursued only for the means of earning a living. If you find yourself at the mercy of the DSS and benefits, use the unconstructive days of unemployment to make a constructive analysis of what you would like to do best and know full well you *can* do. If there are absolutely no openings for your particular talents and abilities yet you know you could go it alone, in a positive manner, having something you *can* offer the public whilst building up a career for yourself, then move heaven and earth to get a loan from a bank so that you can launch yourself in your own venture.

This is the positive approach. Many shops, supermarkets, hairdressing salons, car maintenance firms, minicab companies, cafés, clubs, restaurants, dress shops, smart boutiques, antique shops, removal firms, radio and television shops, jewellers, household and domestic stores, in *your* district alone, have come into existence by one person making the most of a particular talent, getting a little capital together and branching out. And all those large and small businesses of an infinite variety you see around you have evolved from *a positive thought held in mind.* That positive thought may have been at the back of the mind for a long time. Suddenly, a kind of desperation has brought it to the surface, nurtured it, and turned it into a reality! It can be done, and you can do it!

5 Not having a job

In some parts of the country youngsters have gone years without getting a job; there is just no work there. Older people who have been made redundant find that age is their biggest stumbling block to being employed again. For such people, resignation to their unemployed state becomes inevitable. It is difficult to keep on hoping day after day that something will turn up. This is when the exercising of positive thought becomes most important. To wake up every morning and not feel depressed at the prospect of another day fruitlessly spent looking for work takes either superhuman effort or a mind working positively.

Before you go to bed at night, set yourself a task for the next day: maybe to go to the library and read a different newspaper to the one you normally take. Look through the craft section to see if there is a new pastime you could interest yourself in. Contact a voluntary organisation; they often need help with fund-raising, or, if they are connected with the disabled or elderly, then drivers are invaluable. Such spare-time activities occasionally lead to full-time employment, but at the very least they can provide you with a sense of purpose. You are doing something, helping somebody and not just mooching aimlessly around the house, worrying and becoming more depressed. Hopefully, by means such as these you will discover *your* hidden talent and eventually may be able to capitalise on it.

There is a market for every single outstanding talent and ability. What better advice can be given than to seize upon this special ability you may well have inherited from parents or grandparents. If it is necessary to have a mundane job by day, spare time and weekends can be spent pursuing the one great thing in life that is a dominant interest. It can be nurtured and developed until the time comes when it can be used in a money-earning occupation.

Let us now examine the mechanics of the *mind*, for the mind, after all, is the human receiver of all thought and the *brain* is the transmitter of all thought that leads to inevitable action. We will sum up this receiving and transmitting phenomena by calling it

THOUGHT TECHNOLOGY

5

THOUGHT TECHNOLOGY –
THE MECHANICS OF THE MIND

Every thought we have is based on past impressions tuned into present conditions with a view to influencing future moves. It governs our emotions, controls our muscular movements, tells us to advance or to retreat, to raise or to lower our voice, to take action or to be inactive.

Thoughts are things. Like radio and sound and vision waves, we cannot see thought waves any more than we can see sound waves. Sound waves and television waves bounce on and off obstacles and are received by radio sets and television sets. Human thought waves bounce off other people but invariably are received by them when they are dynamic and deliberately aimed *at* them.

While thoughts are invisible, the transmitter of these projected thoughts is encased within the skull and it is, of course, the brain, a very physical thing indeed. It is a miracle of cells that controls our every thought, word, action and emotion. It controls the look in our eyes, the expression on our face, the twist or droop or smile of the lips, the action of our limbs. It is the source of our intelligence and intellect. It is the organ that houses those cells that creates all of our abilities. Some cells suddenly spring to life and we discover a talent we had no idea we possessed. 'I never thought I could do *that*', we exclaim and if we are sensible we at once start to develop that newly found talent. A woman of 60 suddenly discovers she can paint in water colours. A man well past 50 writes a novel out of the blue and it enters the best-seller lists. A fellow in his thirties takes to the stage and is well on the way to becoming an established actor. A teenager suddenly finds he has a brilliant brain for computation. The list is endless. Ancient phrenologists declared that parts of the brain developed and controlled certain talents and abilities. Modern neurological science has discovered this to be true.

Thought technology is the understanding, the control and the practical use, manipulation and development of thoughts and the positive projection of them to others in order to get them to do what we want them to do and to consider us when we want them to consider us. It is the ability to project positive thoughts to others about ourselves that will be favourably received and quickly acted upon.

Other people have brains too. They may well set up resistance to our projected thought waves. We may say to someone: 'I don't suppose you want to go out, do you?' That is a negative thought wave put into words. The immediate reaction may be: 'No, I certainly do not want to go out'. We have put the negative thought into that person's mind and, of course, he will react readily by declaring his wish *not* to go out.

On the other hand, and using the power of positive thought (thought technology in action), we say 'I am sure you want to go out, don't you?' The reaction may well be totally different. The positive thought has been projected and the positive response will be forthcoming. And the reason is really quite simple. The person spoken to and invited to go out has received the positive suggestion and does not wish to appear negative. A positive response, therefore, is given.

That simple little example can be applied to far bigger and far more important things in life when positive thought is called into action. The salesman or woman will say to a prospective customer: 'I don't expect you will be interested in this particular product, will you?' Of course the customer, not wishing to appear unsophisticated or unknowledgeable about that product will say, 'No, I would not be interested in it'. Result: no sale. The salesman who, on the other hand, says, 'I am sure someone of your vision will be interested in this product' flatters the customer by suggesting they are a person of foresight and will want to know more about the product. Result: a sale, and goodwill sown into the bargain.

Thought technology involves an understanding of other people's minds as well as an understanding of the mechanics of our own minds. We must remember what *our* reactions have been when negative thoughts have been projected towards us. We will then be able to recognise the reactions of others to similar negative thoughts projected towards them, very possibly by ourselves.

Thought technology also includes control over our own opinions of ourselves and an understanding of our emotions that prevents us from letting them run away with us and influence our judgement. It is confidence in our own convictions and a respect for our individual opinions, a respect that does not permit others exerting negative influences over them. Many people are fearful of expressing a positive opinion that clashes with the opinions and ideas of others. Thought technology teaches that our own opinions deserve to be aired, even when they appear to be in direct opposition to others. Common sense should prevail in order that personal presumption and a self-opinionated attitude do not compel us to be arrogant and egotistical for the sake of winning an argument or coming out on top. Individualism and originality are respected insofar as it is practical and reasonable. Your individual powers of clear, positive thinking will help you to override others when the situation calls for this, without presenting an unfavourable aspect of yourself. Cool, calm thinking accompanied by a firm conviction that you are right will win the day.

Thought technology also includes positive forward planning that successfully precludes haphazard thought, rash decisions and pre-cipitate actions. It also involves the art of not appearing to be too compliant and menial in order that others should not be able to ride roughshod over you. Being *too* nice can often mean being too negative.

Many men and women shape and form their lives under the cloak of convention, for it seems far safer and convenient to swim with the tide, to move with the crowd, to say what is expected and to do what is 'the thing to do'. This is negative thinking very much in action. Often it is far easier to be conventional than to be unconventional and to stand out on one's own. This makes other people more powerful in the projection of their thoughts towards you and prob-ably in their subsequent actions.

Technology is an understanding of, and the practice of, various sciences which include medicine, psychology, psychiatry, space exploration, nuclear physics and so on. It also results in expertise in the arts, music, painting, graphic design, sculpting, writing, fashion design and creativity and productivity of all and everything that makes life pleasant and progressive.

Thought is the controlling factor of every individual's existence. Therefore thought technology is the understanding and the practice of the mind in action.

Think of the thousand-and-one thoughts you have every hour of every day. Shall I do this, say that, look at the other? Did I do this, that or the other? Was I at fault or was it the other person? Can I be this, that or the other? Why do I continually think of what happened in the past and fear it will upset the present and damage my future?

Are those pains in my chest, in my back, in my head, harmful? Could I have a heart attack, pneumonia, congestion of the lungs? Is lumbago or sciatica overtaking me at long last? Should I get this, that or the other pill or medication from my doctor?

These are all negative distortions and misuse and abuse of the power of positive thought.

They are the spanners thrown into the technological works of logical thinking. Cool, calm and collected thought overcomes the confused, complexed, compulsive mind that results in the defeatist, the hypochondriac, the personality immersed in failure having a permanent fixation with negative thinking.

That is by no means *you*, otherwise you would not be reading this book!

Or *is* it you?

If you can specialise rather than generalise then you are well on the way to being a positive thinker, as we shall see.

6

IT'S POSITIVE TO SPECIALISE

You can specialise in two ways. The two different ways should synchronise the one with the other in order to make a complete and a positive unit.

1 You can specialise in being one sort of person.
2 You can specialise in one certain talent or ability.

1 The person should be compatible with the talent or ability.
2 The ability or talent should mirror the person.

1 The person (personality) should not be at variance with the talent.
2 The talent must not cancel out the person or personality.

Confused? Then let us simplify.

It means, for example, that if the particular talent or ability you have discovered or decided you possess clashes with your personality you will have some difficulty in making the most of that talent and promoting it to its uttermost.

People expect us to behave in a certain way, a way that is compatible with our job or profession. A student, art teacher, actor or pop star can dress exactly as they please and no one will criticise. In fact, comment often arises when they do not dress as we think they should. We expect them to be outlandish or bizarre in their dress, wearing colours that clash, clothes of any fashion or design and mixing styles that do not 'go' together. But as soon as that student leaves college and enters a 'respectable' profession, maybe becoming a banker or a solicitor, then the dress must change too. The person inside will have the same colourful, eccentric personality they possessed in their student days, but in order to be successful, they must outwardly change, at least during their working week, to suit the image their customers or clients will have of them.

In a similar manner, taking it that your capabilities lie in scenic design in the world of the stage, films or television, a dull, colourless, unprepossessing personality would not synchronise with the outward-thinking, creative person usually associated with the production of brilliant stage décor, theatrical costumes and studio sets.

What you know you can do well should excite you to the point that you *become* the sort of person that other people expect you to be. Your attitude should inspire others to regard you as a specialist in your particular chosen career. You must *be* what your job *is*. If your personality seems to contradict your job in life it tends to rob onlookers of faith and confidence in you and in your ability to be of service to them. Those students who have become bankers will have to leave a good deal of their exuberant eccentricity in the wardrobe along with their weekend clothes if they wish those they do business with to have complete confidence in them. This does not mean they must become dull, negative personalities, but it does mean recognising that the general public will have their own perception of bankers and that they must fill that prescribed role.

Consider these few examples of people whose careers or vocations synchronise with their particular personalities, thereby making them acceptable to others who need their services; the seeds of confidence are therefore securely sown.

The priest
He (or she) exudes a sense of comfort and succour, offers hope to the hopeless, forgiveness to the sinful, faith to the faithless.

The doctor
His (or her) calm attitudes soothe away fears of illness and offer renewed hope. His confident manner often produces immediate feelings of relief and well-being in patients. In hospitals at the bedside he encourages hopes of speedy recovery and eradicates fears of operations.

The psychologist or the psychiatrist
He (or she) settles the confused and fearful mind, soothes away negative thoughts of the past, brightens the present and gives hope for the future.

In each case, the personality fits the job and the person is in perfect synchronisation with the specialist outlook.

This projection of positive thought in combination with the particular job in life produces a complete entity that spells success and confidence and encourages confidence in others.

That principle should be applied to all careers, from the lawyer to the solicitor to the estate agent, the lecturer, the writer, the journalist, the nutritionist, the teacher and tutor, the sales manager, the sales representative, the Member of Parliament and so on.

It's just great to specialise in one thing, instead of knowing something about lots of things but being of little good in any of them! A smattering of knowledge about a variety of subjects produces the haphazard person whose positive thinking prowess is so diffused as to render their personality equally so. This lack of synchronised thought is bewildering to onlookers and produces the much-clichéd 'Jack of all trades and master of none'.

The war-cry of the positive thinker is: 'I know what I want and I mean to get it'.

And when the personality fits the chosen desire in life, invariably positive thinkers *do* get what they want.

Apart from the fact that positive thinking strengthens mental and emotional output it also adds life and vitality to the body, as we shall see in the following chapter.

7

THE POWER OF THOUGHT GIVES STRENGTH TO THE BODY

Think big and you can *be* big. Think strong and you can *be* strong. In a few simple examples let us see how the power of positive thought can add strength to physical endeavours; how it can prevent you from feeling inadequate when it comes to performing normal, average feats of strength, from carrying a child to pushing a heavy load; how it can help you control your breathing or talking and walk with an air of command.

There are times in our lives when we admit to being surprised by our own strength. They are often quite unimportant, but we seem to have tapped reserves of strength that we never knew we possessed. Perhaps a child had grown tired of walking and had asked to be carried. All was well at first, but the child grew heavier and heavier the further you went. You could not put them down because they had fallen asleep. But somehow you managed to struggle on, arms at breaking point, until you reached home. Because you knew that there was no alternative, your thought processes took over and persuaded your body that it could cope, it was strong enough for the task in hand, and it worked.

It may be your lot when gardening to have to push a wheelbarrow full of earth from one part of the garden to another. Or maybe your car has broken down in the street and has to be pushed round a corner into a quiet side turning. Concentrate all your thinking power down both arms into both hands as they grip the heavy object to be shifted. Think extra power into your shoulders as well, into the muscles of your stomach, into your thighs and your lower legs. Let your feet, also, feel the extra power seeping into them. With this picture held in mind, push with the combined strength of your body and your mind, visualise the heavy load moving at your command. We all know that crisis lends strength to the body when dire occasions demand, and so it can be in a non-critical situation. A strong mind in a strong body forms a wonderful partnership.

Sometimes you may experience difficulty in breathing normally, particularly when faced with making an important decision, or during a confrontation with a belligerent protagonist, or at a vital interview. Given normal good health and freedom from any respiratory problems or blood-pressure difficulties, you can control your breathing in any crisis by imagining it to be functioning normally. This can be established by concentrating your powers of positive thought into your lungs and into your respiratory tract in a matter of seconds, visualising your lungs strongly inhaling and exhaling air and by willing your breathing to calm down and to resume its normal pace. In doing this as quickly and as effectively as possible you will prevent your words from becoming strangled and unintelligible, so giving your enemy of the moment the impression you are weak, frightened and confused. Mind-controlled breathing by this method will help you to impress a prospective employer or the senior spokesperson at an important interview that you are cool, calm and able to collect your wits. In a crisis, an accident, the sudden illness of a friend, a sudden unnerving confrontation, this method of mind-controlled breathing will save you from precipitate panic.

We breathe as we think. When we think normally, we breathe normally.

Think of the Shakespearian speech on the battlefield: '*When the blast of war breaks out – summon up the blood, stiffen the sinews – lend to the eye a terrible aspect!*'

All instant, positive thought power must be directed to the body, the limbs, the lungs, the heart and to the eyes.

When we think abnormally we tend to breathe abnormally. But not so if and when we allow the mind to take over.

Firm, strong strides when walking lend to the body a sense of purpose. We are going somewhere, not shuffling off here, there, or anywhere. Mind power directed to the body when walking commands the legs to stride out, the arms to swing, the head to be held high, the chest to expand, the stomach to be held in. Misdirected mind power tells the body to shuffle along on heavy legs, head bent to the ground, arms lifeless by the side.

We cannot ever dismiss the power of the mind over the body.

Let me relate to you the following personal instance which has an enormous bearing on the power of the mind over the body. During the Second World War my wife was having our first child, a daughter. I was rushed to the Military Hospital with congestion of the lungs at the very time my wife was giving birth. Naturally, I wished for compassionate leave to go home to see my wife and newly-born daughter. But when a nurse took my temperature, it was 101° and therefore I could not be discharged from hospital.

I asked the nurse to take my temperature again, half-an-hour later. When it was taken, I had willed it down, by the power of positive thought, to the normal 98.4°. Two hours later I was on a train back to my family.

Another and even more striking example of the power of mind over body was illustrated in another incident which involved me being in hospital, this time in 1985, with pneumonia. After that condition had been cured, a scan revealed that my kidneys were in pretty bad condition. A sympathetic woman doctor whispered words such as 'kidney failure' and 'dialysis'. She went on her way round the wards leaving me in considerable trepidation. However, there was a week in which to think over the crisis situation which had suddenly arisen. Then there was another scan and afterwards a length period of waiting.

Shortly afterwards, however, the doctor came to my bed, her eyes wide open.

'What on *earth* have you done to your kidneys?' she asked. 'When you came into hospital you had a high fever and your kidneys were in a very bad state. Now, they are perfectly normal again!' I was discharged from hospital a few days later, and there has been no recurrence of the trouble. (Touch wood.)

The time between the first and second scan was spent, not in worrying over the fate that appeared to have struck, but in having the positive conviction that it was not acceptable and that the mind had to *do* something about it.

And it did. In no uncertain manner!

In many instances, the mind *can* cure the body when sufficient positive thought is directed to it. Feelings of utter desolation and resignation can so often make a condition much worse and bring on additional symptoms that further lower the body's resistance until it succumbs completely to the illness from which it appears to be suffering.

Hope springs eternal, provided the mind wills it to be so.

Have you ever thought of your brain as being something far more dynamic than merely a mass of jangled and criss-crossed nerves and cells? It is, in fact, a very complex thinking machine.

8

THE THINKING MACHINE

The brain, our thinking machine, directs our use of free will, our intelligence and intellect, our consciousness, and subconsciousness, and the vagaries of our emotions.

The emotions are experiences of states of mind which have strong feelings about or reactions to what we do, say or think. Emotions constitute a conscious state which brings out dominant positive or negative characteristics. You laugh or cry, run away or stay to fight. Emotions are thoughts that dominate present moves based on past happy or unhappy, successful or unsuccessful circumstances and conditions. There are the emotions of fright, confidence in adversity, joy and happiness.

All are products of the thinking machine – the brain and the mind in action.

The thinking machine also produces instincts based on the responses to which you have been conditioned in earlier days and to which you react when similar conditions arise. Instincts are very much dominated by common sense and the vital desire for self-preservation. Instincts are closely allied to feelings and emotions. The power of positive thinking depends to a great degree on feelings and emotions as they colour and affect present moves.

Hysteria is an emotion that is out of control. We may scream or laugh in an uncontrollable manner when faced with a sudden frightful sight or when we suffer a shock of some sort or the other. Negative thought steps in immediately and the main defence against the 'horror' expresses itself in an audible display of sound: laughter, crying, unintelligible speech, in order to counter and to relieve the suddenly attacked conditions of normal calmness and peace of mind. Alternatively, the defence reaction may express itself by hitting out, by attacking or producing a flow of invective. When these audible, visible and demonstrative reactions have exhausted themselves the subject becomes calm again, positive thought takes over and a solution to the particular problem then begins to formulate itself in the brain.

With many of us it is impossible for positive thought to take over until we *have* surrendered to our emotions of horror or hysteria. It is a cathartic experience; giving way to hysteria seems to cleanse the emotions and allow rational thought to take over once we have calmed down. There are differing degrees of hysteria; while one person, who is normally level-headed, breaks down into uncontrollable sobbing, another, who is more volatile, will rant and rave and even throw things. As long as it does no lasting harm to those close to us, giving way to these emotions can be a way of lifting a burden and finding a solution to a problem.

When positive thinking finally takes over, bright sunshine starts to melt away the misty clouds of fearful thought and reason once more reigns supreme.

Human nature so very often refuses to accept thoughts of fear or personal tragedy. The mind takes refuge in non-acceptance of such facts for a brief period and a breakdown may result. Enforced rest, hospitalisation, medication or psychiatric treatment make the sufferer the centre of attention. Waking from this period of deliberate mental and physical retreat the patient finally arises, refreshed, thinking more clearly and prepared to accept what has happened and to tackle the problem in a positive frame of mind.

On the other hand, the strong-minded individual, the person who thinks positively all of the time, does not revert to hysteria or to the breakdown syndrome. He or she refuses to be adversely influenced by or negatively affected by bad news, physical disaster or major upsets and rises to the occasion with the thinking machine on red alert to accept, adapt, apply and overcome.

For such people nature's self-defence against trial and tribulation does not have to take over. In fact, a challenge in time of crisis revitalises the mind and the body. The adrenalin rises, positive thinking crowds in, dismissing all negative thoughts, and preparations are quickly made to tackle the trouble.

How does your thinking machine react in times of crisis?

If a fire starts on your premises, would you:

> Panic and run?
>
> Warn others in the house?
>
> Try to tackle the blaze?
>
> Dial 999?

If you lose your job, would you:

> Blame your boss?
>
> Blame yourself?
>
> Accept you were in the wrong?
>
> Resign yourself to the dole queue?
>
> Soon look for another job?

If you witness a bad street accident, would you:

> Run away from the sight?
>
> Feel sick?
>
> Faint?
>
> Dial 999?
>
> Give immediate assistance?

If you witness a mugging or a robbery, would you:

> Turn and walk away?
>
> Try to tackle the attacker?
>
> Report the matter at once?

If a loved one suddenly leaves you for someone else, would you:

> Wallow in self-pity?
>
> Try to avenge the intruder in your affair or marriage?
>
> Decide you will never allow yourself to become involved again?

Count your past blessings and happy moments and look for someone else?

If you fail a vital exam, would you:

Decide not to sit the exam ever again?

Consider yourself an abject failure?

Re-enrol for the same subject again?

Try for something else quite different?

If you suffer an accident that impairs your working ability, would you:

Resign yourself to being useless for life?

Invest in creative and productive activities in tune with your capabilities?

No score for that quiz for it is only too apparent which are the negative reactions and which are the positive ones.

The law of compensation invariably takes over when disasters arise. There is always a positive factor in all negative situations. It is up to you, the positive manipulator of your own personal thinking machine, to find them.

For every minus there is an undoubted plus. We read about them in the newspapers every day. Triumphs over accidents, crippling illnesses, bereavements, the downfalls of industrial moguls, wrecked marriages, wrecked careers. The list of personal misfortunes is endless. Yet positive-thinking people rise above them all and direct their thoughts into other channels that so very often well and truly compensate for their misfortunes.

You, too, can do the same, in the unhappy circumstance of fate dealing you an unkind blow.

Some people only think in a positive way when at work, involved in business deals, concentrating on earning the daily bread. But the power of positive thinking should also be extended to the domestic scene. At home, a great deal of negative thinking often goes on because people relax and use the home as a stage for releasing negative feelings and frustrations. But such negative attitudes are hardly conducive to a happy family atmosphere. In the following chapter you will see exactly why.

9

POSITIVE THINKING HELPS THE HOME SCENE

Whether you are married or single, positive attitudes towards those around you in the family scene help to build harmonious relationships which, in turn, are reflected in your day-to-day work so that you beaver away happily and efficiently and look forward to your return home each evening.

If you are a parent, ask yourself the following questions:

As a parent are you:

> Obsessed with too much convention?

> Far too strict?

> Overproud of your offspring?

> Apt to spoil them?

Do you think your children are:

> For ever young?

> Irresponsible and too self-willed?

> Unable to fend for themselves successfully?

Do you give your offspring:

> Too much licence?

> Too much pocket money?

> Too much unnecessary supervision?

As a parent, are you apt to be jealous:

> Of your son as a growing lad?

> Of your daughter as a growing girl?

As a parent do you:

> Continually make 'in my day' comments?

> Make your children feel inadequate?

> Inhibit their self-confidence and desire for independence?

Negative attitudes like these tend to set your offspring against you and sow seeds of revolt in the boy or the girl. Children subjected to such attitudes on the part of parents tend to grow up in an atmosphere of manufactured resentment and revolt and could easily lead to their being negatively minded themselves in their teens and adult life. On the other hand, children brought up in such a domestic atmosphere might develop an offensive attitude towards others in later life as a defensive reaction *against* life.

We have an image of the Victorian domestic scene as repressive, but children in the last century were often just as much a source of worry and concern to their parents as they are today. The problems may have been different ones to those experienced by parents now, but the depth of concern was the same.

Each generation views its parents and children in much the same light whatever the age they live in is like – whether repressive or permissive. Parents think their children are not respectful enough, want their own way too often, grow up too quickly and want freedom to go their own way too early in life. Children think their parents are out of step with the times and fashions, show too much concern for their welfare, try to tell them what to do and make them into younger copies of themselves.

All that is needed for harmonious living is a lot of give and take on all sides, surrender on the little things so that the more important issues can be discussed rationally. Things will not always work out neatly, but if you remember to apply positive thinking to every situation you should achieve the best outcome possible for all concerned. It may not always be the one you would have liked, but a compromise solution is better than a complete victory as this can lead to bitterness and resentment on the part of the person who lost that particular encounter.

Parents have had more experience of life than their children; they should also remember how they felt when trying to win over their own parents to a revolutionary new idea. Their children's choice of music, clothes, hobbies, friends and behaviour may be completely at variance with their own, but they should feel some satisfaction that their offspring have the confidence to be individuals rather than safe carbon copies of themselves.

The most important thing to remember is to be positive at all times. Negative attitudes often produce negative results in the young mind that foster frustrated and inhibited attitudes which, in turn, may produce the teenager in revolt.

10

THOUGHT TECHNOLOGY IN ACTION

As stated in Chapter Five, thought technology is the understanding, control, manipulation and development of thoughts and the positive projection of those thoughts to others in order to influence them to stop, look and listen to you. It should also make you examine yourself in order to readjust your thinking processes so that they work *for* you rather than *against* you.

Now let us take thought technology a stage further in order to make it a positive influence in our lives.

A determination to understand, control and develop our thoughts should result in the ability to:

discriminate in order to make the correct decisions;

appreciate contrasts and weigh them one against the other;

concentrate on a given job at a given time;

form positive judgments as a natural reaction to crises;

overcome negative opposition from others;

recognise right from wrong without hesitation.

A step further in this positive direction will help you to rid yourself for all time of the four 'Damnable Ds':

Depression

Defeatism

Despondency

Doubts

. . . and to recognise, in your character and personality, the four 'Exaggerated Es', which are:

Egotism

Embarrassment

Evasiveness

Excesses

The final results of these applications of thought technology will result in a firm resolve to overcome:

fear of failure;

impulsive actions;

guilt feelings caused by past errors.

In addition, these applications of thought technology will alert you to the immediate rejection of:

over-emphasizing the importance of the past;

desire for protection from adversity;

frustration in the face of opposition;

indecision when faced with difficult problems;

obsessive rituals born of anxiety;

compulsive obstinacy in the face of common sense;

overweaning and false pride and vanity;

unfair and unnecessary prejudices;

reticence or deliberate evasiveness in the face of reason;

self-righteousness;

self-adoration or self-deprecation.

What a devastating list of potential human failings!

But we are all prone to them from time to time, or, indeed, for a whole lifetime if we are not fully in control of our power of thought.

Here are three case histories from my files to which the technique of thought technology was applied, resulting in the conversion of negative thought to positive thought to the patient's benefit.

Case history 1

The patient writes: 'I am in a constant state of fear. Fear of almost everything and everyone. I wake each morning with a feeling of foreboding. This stays with me most of the day and, although my office duties are comparatively light, I get home in the evenings feeling quite exhausted.'

Thought technology discovered that the patient had been brought up by strict parents and was reliant on them for advice as to what to do and what not to do, with the result that the child became over-dependent on them and found it impossible to make any material, emotional or physical moves on her own without first consulting them. Up to the age of 18 she was rarely able to go out by herself for fear of accidents or unpleasant incidents occurring. These fears had been fostered in her mind by her over-strict parents constantly warning her of the evils that might befall her. Through thought technology she learnt the power of positive thought and its ability to cancel out the negative suggestions put into her mind by her unwise and overbearing parents. She surrounded herself, then, by a pro-tective shield of positivism that she successfully imagined as a very real influence round her physical and emotional selves – a sort of mental 'guardian angel'. Eventually she was able to face up to the busy world of crowded streets and confusing transport. In the final stages of her treatment she woke refreshed in the morning and really looking forward to the adventures of the day and to what possible pleasures, rather than fears, might lie ahead of her each day.

Case history 2

The patient writes: 'Ever since I was a child I have been unable to swallow aspirin or any type of tablet or capsule easily. My throat always seems to close up, its muscles tightening in resistance against swallowing the object. Often I am sick as the result of trying to take it down. Soluble tablets are, of course, an excellent substitute for me and I have no problems with them. But not all tablets are made in soluble form and unfortunately most of those prescribed for me by my doctor are not soluble.'

Thought technology taught this patient, at the age of 23, to visualise her throat remaining open and perfectly relaxed each time she had to swallow a tablet or a capsule. She was told to think of her throat as a wide, open tube a few moments before taking the tablet and, as she placed the object in her mouth, to think of it going down her throat smoothly and easily, to follow, in her mind's eye, the journey of the tablet as it slid, nicely, smoothly and easily down. She was also to think of the water she was taking as washing the tablet or capsule down without any trouble whatsoever. After quite a few attempts at this concentration of thought power on to her throat she was at last able to swallow the medication with ease and her problem was solved.

Case history 3

The patient writes: 'Many years ago I had a stomach operation that frightened me very much. I often sleep badly at night, feeling convinced the old trouble is flaring up again, that pains are starting in my stomach. I then breathe with difficulty and sometimes sleep evades me for the remainder of the night. This has now become a regular occurrence, at the age of 40, and I feel sure the pains and the breathlessness mean I will have to have another operation.'

Thought technology discovered that the operation that had taken place many years previously was a definite one-off and that it was completely impossible for the old trouble to arise again. The patient was advised of this and it was confirmed by the doctor. The pains were purely psychosomatic, brought on by the old memories of the fright at discovering the operation had to take place. This was made known to the patient and it was emphasized that the imagined pains and the subsequent breathlessness only occurred at night, while in bed, and while the body was at its lowest state of resistance. The mind tended to give way to imagined fears and frightened memories of the past. The fears and pains and breathing difficulties never arose in daytime when the patient was gainfully employed. The breathlessness at night arose only from the false conviction that the stomach pains were occurring again. It was 'fear-breathing'. This had happened to the patient from the moment the illness was diagnosed, a state that remained, on and off, right up to the operation and which started again several years later. The patient was taught how to relax at night, to think hard about the stomach being totally devoid of the offending tissue that had made the operation necessary in the first place, to realise how easy it now was, and had been for years after the operation, to eat and to drink normally. The power of positive thought was to be directed to the stomach each night like a powerful laser beam, soothing away negative fears and consequently the pains. In addition, the patient was told that the breathing difficulties would completely disappear because the fear-thoughts about the stomach would become non-existent. The advice was successful after a very short time and the problems ceased to exist.

The mind has a powerful influence on the body. Many hours after a visit to the dentist, when we are lying quietly in bed, we believe we can still feel the drill working on our tooth. It is quite common for people who have had a leg amputated to believe that they still have the limb. They are sure they can feel some sensation in it. This must be the mind refusing to believe the leg has gone. It has been there for 50 or 60 years so where is it now? It isn't logical. The body must wait for the mind to accept the fact that the leg has been amputated before the sensation will cease.

11

THOUGHT POWER IN VISION AND CREATIVITY

If you have vision, the imaginative perception of ideas, then you can visualise and create something quite out of the ordinary. You may have a strong urge to create something in an art form or a mechanical, electronic or computerised form.

Not many people realise that, among the many, many brain cells they possess are cells that, in a lifetime, are never brought into action. It is perfectly logical to state that an office worker, an electrical engineer, a builder, decorator, salesman, doctor or lawyer could, if they wished, employ a different part of the brain and start an entirely new career. But safety in a job, the receipt of a regular income, security and the promise of a pension later on forbids exploration into the possibility of other, perhaps more exciting, outlets and endeavours.

Nevertheless, there *are* people who *do* get exciting little twinges from time to time that make them think there could be something else to life, something else they could do in addition to their daily grind or as a substitute for a boring and ill-rewarded job or one they realise they are not suited for.

They may suddenly have a vision. It may be connected with the arts – painting, sculpting, drawing, designing, fashion designing, stage and film design, musical composition, acting, film, theatre or stage direction. Or it may involve inventions, like computers, electrical gadgets, domestic appliances, cars and so on. Such thoughts and visions indicate the stirrings of undiscovered brain cells that can be brought into use to create those very things that are beginning to become constant and pushy little visions in the mind.

The positive-thinking man or woman does not easily dismiss these urgent promptings of a desire to create something unconnected with their everyday pursuit. Indeed, the particular brain cell that is suddenly prompting the idea will not easily go away and most likely will go on and on niggling away in the mind until such time as some definite action is taken. In spite of the daily job or the pursuit of a particular career, imagine the secret pleasure of the dawning of a new vision, the creation of a new activity in life that these promptings could cause.

What could be more exciting in the journey to work and the journey back again than to visualise a brand-new concept, a great new ambition, a fresh outlet to life. Copious notes, scribbled doodles and rough plans, hours spent in pleasurable visualisation as the brain goes on insisting and insisting that this new idea should be realised and finally become fact. That is the stuff of which life is made for the thoughtful person. Its very daring and originality may take your breath away at first as your compare it with the mundane life you lead at the moment.

Whatever this striking new ambition, this brand-new vision may be, providing you are positive-minded about it, there is no reason whatsoever why you cannot follow through and turn visualisation into realisation from this very moment on.

Remember:

That which is *visualised* can be *realised*.

Positive thought projected in a positive manner gains attention from others who can help you with your new ambitions.

Positive thought is the *confident* thought – the 'I am' thought.

All men are equal, but many have to be led. You will become a leader in your new concept.

And . . . :

If you can see a thing in your mind's eye, you can achieve it.

Think *success* and you will *gain* success.

Think you will be what you want to be, and will accomplish what you wish to accomplish.

Believe in what you want and you will have it:

See it.

Feel it.

Want it.

Desire it.

Attract it.

Get it.

The magnetism of desire is a most powerful factor in life. Without it, the creative impulse or the power of visualisation, how could the world progress any further? Each day, hidden brain cells are thrusting themselves into the daylight of living and insisting on being recognised – and used.

If one of your undiscovered brain cells suddenly leaps into action do not lightly dismiss its insistence. Probably you have already wondered, could I do this, that or the other? Could I create this or that? Could I write a novel, paint a picture, play a part on stage, write a television script? Sometimes an unused brain cell lies dormant for ever. At other times, and with other people, it is forced to come to the surface to be exploited to the full.

How about *you*?

What creative thing could *you* visualise and bring into being?

Do give it some thought. Something *is* there waiting to be discovered.

12

THOUGHT POWER TO FIGHT STRESS

Stress means *distress*. Stress is very often brought about by perceptions of a given situation that become emotionally discoloured by negative attitudes and unnecessary fears. Stress may well be useful in times of crisis when it stirs the adrenal glands into positive action to fight rather than to run away. That sort of stress soon gives way to a determination to confront the problem and overcome it.

That, of course, is good.

But negative, sustained stress is the enemy that requires strong thought power to overcome it, to put it into correct perspective in order that it does not colour a situation with such hopelessness that the situation becomes truly negative and therefore practically unsolvable.

Sustained stress can often become the reason for a nervous breakdown which, in turn, becomes the escape route to avoiding having to solve a problem or meeting a dangerous situation head on.

Stress often results from a 'Shall I – shan't I' situation in which two opposing ideas produce a stalemate which can offer no solution either way.

Stress symptoms can often be brought on if you find your life is:

monotonous

unproductive

going nowhere

undervalued

unintelligible

precarious

dishonest

repetitive

Each one of the above states produces emotional unrest and negative convictions that all is not right with your world. The decision to accept them rather than to exchange them for better things further develops your stress symptoms to the point where they can become obsessional. Fear of failure follows. This outlook can pretty soon become a very real fact. You then fall into a stressful state that produces the following side effects:

Things easily hurt your feelings, almost reduce you to tears.

You find it hard to recall details.

Crowds begin to confuse you.

There is never enough time in which to do everything.

You suffer loss of appetite.

You cannot sleep well at night, and feel weary during the day.

You feel exhausted when you rise, unable to face your day.

All this because one of these emotional states of a negative kind colours your daily existence.

Why put up with this?

There are few situations in life that cannot be solved by positive thought power if you accept that it is just as easy to face up to and to overcome stress as it is to fall victim to it.

Almost everyone has someone in life they are living for. It can be a husband, a wife, a father, a mother, sister or brother, very close friend or a lover. They respect you, and expect you to live up to their expectations.

Why let them and yourself down at the same time?

Live for them as undoubtedly they live for *you*. Be embarrassed and ashamed to go under, for their sakes.

Make them your target for ultimate success in overcoming whatever is causing you your distress. Your enemies in life are their enemies also. Your problems are their problems. Talk over your troubles with them. Tell them what you think. Let their positive thoughts overcome your negative ones.

Indulge yourself in frequent relaxation sessions, accompanied by controlled breathing. Breathe in negative thoughts relative to your stress state and breathe out positive decisions to solve your stress state. Let each outward breath cancel out each negative inward breath. Remember how difficult and restricted breathing occurred when you were faced with the condition that first caused your stress state? Relax pleasurably, now, in a state of steady, natural, controlled breathing as you review the situation step-by-step, making firm decisions and formulating a positive programme of action that will help you over your present stressful situation. Do this often. If you can visualise an end to the crisis then you now know that you can *realise* it, in the long run.

And, if you happen to be a loner, what then?

If no one depends on you, and you depend on no one, just remember that you depend *upon yourself*. *You* are as important as anyone else.

You were not put into the world by your parents to have to depend on the vagaries of other humans. Even if they are separated, divorced or have died, you owe it to yourself to keep your self-respect or to regain it if you have lost it.

Think upwards and outwards rather than downwards and inwards. Relax and breathe yourself into a positive stage of mind so that you do not allow a stress state to develop into a nervous breakdown.

Lots of men and women do, but you do not have to be one of them. Whatever your age, there is hope ahead for you.

Use the technology of thought that has already been explained to you in this book to help you combat stress and to win through. God helps those who help themselves, remember. Do not resign yourself to a fate that really does not have to exist at all.

It is really not enough just to think about yourself: how you look, how you dress, how you speak, the opinions you have about yourself. If you want others to look at you, pay attention to you and be aware of you, it is important to learn just how to project yourself to them by positive thought power.

13

PROJECT YOUR THOUGHT POWER

Project an image of your face, the way in which you dress, how you move, your habits, character and personality.

Project a lasting impression of your voice, its tonal qualities.

The other person receives these impressions of *you*, responds to *your* 'signature tune', taking in those images, impressions and sounds and filing them away for future reference so that they can be drawn upon again whenever necessary.

As soon as we meet someone for the first time we make an impression, but the sort of impression we make is in our control. If we send out positive thought waves by being constructive and open in our outlook on life they will be well received. So remember, when you are next introduced to someone, you have the power to imprint a positive picture of yourself. This is important as we are so often told that first impressions count.

This picture should be as powerful as you can make it so that whenever your new acquaintance recalls the meeting he or she will have a strong feeling about you because of what you said, how you looked and what you thought on that first occasion.

Our lives are controlled to a very great extent by the feelings other people have for us. And if we feed them the right information then their reaction to us will be just what we want it to be.

Don't forget, of course, that others may be using the very same tactics, so be well prepared to counter any negative thought waves that may be directed towards yourself.

Our emotions are controlled by what we see, think and feel about others immediately involved in our lives and by what *they* see, think and feel about *us*. The technique of thought projection involves our getting there first with our own positive thought projection if there is a conflict of personalities. No one is independent. Everyone depends upon someone else. The most anti-social person in the world depends upon others – *to leave him or her alone.*

The happiest people are those who, by positive thought projection, make lasting good impressions upon others and upon those on whom they depend. They know the magic of thought power and make the very most of it.

The power of thought is undoubtedly very great, sometimes uncannily so, for many people have experienced the phenomenon of sudden telepathic thoughts. It may be that if we were unable to communicate by speech our telepathic powers would develop to such an extent that communication by thought processes would become more common.

Happily, we are all able to speak and to convey thoughts and ideas and impressions to others. Speech plus thought projection therefore constitutes a very powerful means of communication.

And we must make the most out of this ideal combination of thoughts and speech. As we grow older we learn the negativity of hate-thoughts, the magic of love-thoughts and we know which words will best express those emotions.

Positive thought projection involves the technique of holding the other person's gaze by looking them straight between the eyes, speaking reasonably slowly and distinctly and with absolute conviction and sincerity.

> Will your personality and conviction to enter the conscious thoughts of your opponent.
>
> Feel your thoughts leaving your mind and, like laser beams, entering the other person's mind.
>
> Underline each positive phrase with appropriate modulation of speech.
>
> Subconsciously will your thoughts to be received by the other person.

This application of thought technology rarely fails. But, *do not*:

> look away from the person while speaking;
>
> distract his or her attention by fiddling with hands or clothes;
>
> speak in a monotonous tone of voice, lacking conviction;
>
> smile in an apologetic manner to save face.

14

YOU CANNOT BE POSITIVE ALL OF THE TIME

If the world were full of positive-minded folk there would be no emotional, industrial, domestic or social conflicts and the world could be a very dull place indeed.

There would be no healthy competition, conflict or mixed emotions. In fact, it is the occasional negative thoughts and emotions that strengthen the desire to *be* positive most of the time in order to produce a properly balance life-programme.

Deliberate attempts to overcome the petty annoyances of daily existence will help to separate the emotions of good and evil, love and hate, ambition and failure. In that way, emotions and attitudes to daily life will become adult, sophisticated and stabilised. No truly convincing personality, adequate and sure of itself, can be formed on emotions that are unsteady or in conflict with each other.

Either one is a yes-man or -woman and negative or one refuses to take 'no' for an answer and is, therefore, positive. Being a yes-man or -woman is to receive all the powerful thought projections of others without demur or argument. The positive thinker analyses, argues, objects, makes counter-suggestions.

The 'not-always-positive person' is apt to be, at one time or another, conscious of feelings of inferiority, inadequacy, or fear. The important thing is that mistakes made through occasional negativity should serve as experiences for the future when positivity finally takes over.

A purposefully cultivated insight into human nature helps one recognise and accept the disposal and the dispersal of positive and negative emotions that make for success or failure. That is, in effect, simple individual psychology that we can all apply to ourselves.

It must be said that the too-positive personality, hell-bent on applying their fixed outlook on fellow beings can quickly fall out of favour. It is the occasional lapse into negative thought that makes them a good example when they suddenly see the light and make positive moves again.

Lots of negative-minded folk drearily ask over and over again the clichéd question, 'What is life?' This dubious question is invariably the query of those individuals who are trying to escape from life and whose positive-mind quota is practically nil. They either have a very gloomy outlook on life, or are drifters or people who feel hard done by. They think the world owes them a living with little or no effort having to be put in on their part. It is only by giving of ourselves that we receive fulfilment in our lives. We must contribute to receive. But all of this requires energy and commitment and it is no failure on our part if we have days or weeks when things go wrong and we find it difficult, maybe even impossible, to summon up the inner resources required to think ourselves positively through the difficult times. It is then we need other positive thinkers around us. We may need to unburden ourselves, but we must choose carefully. Negative thinkers will be no help at all and will, in fact, make us feel a good deal worse by piling all their gloomy prophecies on to our already problematical situation.

By contrast, how very pleasant *not* to be one of those unfortunates. How pleasant, in fact, to be *you*.

For you see life in its correct perspective. You approach life with a sense of realism. But you allow yourself an extravagance from time to time just to add a bit more colour to life, to add exoticism and excitement, warmth and a sense of humour, maybe a touch of cynicism, a satirical slant here and there.

You look at life with intelligence and intellect. You are aware of opportunity tempting and titillating. You welcome those around you who excite your senses when they reach your emotional depths.

Unlike the philosophers of gloom, you know what life is. You know it to be a sense of positive awareness, a lively acknowledgement of existence, a meeting place of desire and fulfilment, of visualisation and realisation, of fantasy and fact.

You know life to be an explosion of mental energy triggered off by the plus and minus, positive and negative elements that complete a circuit of thought and accomplishment. The driving force of the positive mind determines:

the direction we take;

how much influence we use when trying to sway others;

our personal happiness and achievement;

the success of our relationships with others;

our attitude to life;

how we express our desires and ambitions.

When you are positive-minded these are the factors you recognise as important and the ones that you try to develop.

In addition, the positive mind's driving force is always there to help you to overcome tension in situations which demand calmness and coolness.

15

THE POWER OF THOUGHT IN TENSE SITUATIONS

Not one person ever completely avoids having to face up to at least a few tension-filled moments in life that call for all the powerful reserves of positive thought to be brought into action in order to fight off the negative thoughts of failure.

Nervous tension very often paralyses the normal functioning of the mind to the extent where you become temporarily confused, mute, immobile, anxiety-ridden and totally incapable of facing up to the physical or emotional crisis that lies ahead.

In learning how to use the power of positive thought in the minor crises you are able, later, to triumph over major adversities that occur from time to time in life.

The application of positive thought power in times of tension is to make sure all negative thoughts of failure or dread of pain or discomfort are eradicated at the outset or as the stress time proceeds. The end product is to clear the mind of thoughts of failure, replacing them with thoughts of conquering the particular problem or malady. The physical self, now armed against bodily and brain anticipation of pain, renews its strength to resist such fear-thoughts. The body builds up a defence mechanism against pain or the fear of pain and is, therefore, better able to cope with discomfort when it actually arises. Psychosomatic suffering or symptomatic pains can be created by negative thoughts where positive thinking would reason that such discomforts and pains do not have to exist at all. Negative thoughts and worries likely to cause failure to pass exams or important interviews do not have to exist at all.

Case 1: A visit to the dentist

Imagine someone with dreadful, persistent toothache for days on end. As the time draws near for the visit to the dentist the pain gradually diminishes. Why is this? It is because the anticipation of the dental surgery, the dentist, the table laid out with gleaming instruments, the jab when the needle goes in, the thought of the pull as the tooth is extracted proves too much for the patient preparing for the visit. The defence mechanism takes over. Suddenly, no pain! Why, therefore, bother to go to the dentist at all? Probably it's only just a cold in the gum. The tooth doesn't really need to be taken out after all. What a relief. But, soon after the decision has been taken not to go to the dentist, that pain returns, just as before. The brain has temporarily deceived the body into not accepting messages of toothache from the bad tooth. It has done this because of fear of the impending visit and probable extraction. Symptoms have vanished for a while, but the cause is, of course, still very much there.

However, positive thinkers will welcome the brief respite from pain, but will not be fooled by it. They will make the journey to the dentist, pleased with the temporary relief from pain, but knowing it to be what it is: merely their brain trying to tell them to put it off. By the time they are in the dentist's chair, pleased with themselves and their firm resolve, they will find that this positive attitude still persists, the pain in the tooth is still relieved and doubtless they will also find their brain now determines to help them overcome the momentary pain of the needle injecting the gums with a local anaesthetic. It will all be over in a few seconds. Out will come the offending tooth with hardly any discomfort and their troubles will be at an end. Having accepted the mental bluff that the tooth no longer hurts, the patient has gone to the dentist after all, as arranged, and to their pleasant surprise has found their positive-minded attitude has allowed their brain to help make the operation as painless as possible. Meanwhile, of course, the negative-minded sufferer has failed to visit the dentist, their toothache has returned and they have got nowhere pretty fast.

Case 2: Awaiting an operation

Even in the case of a minor operation, such as when suffering from a hernia or cataracts, apprehension while awaiting admission to hospital can be considerable. The mind revolves around the anti-septic smells of the hospital ward, thoughts of the anaesthetic being administered, the surgeon's knife or the laser beam penetrating the flesh and the mind squirms at such thoughts even though the patient knows they will feel nothing. In cases of far more serious operations the mind can wreak havoc on the patient, so reducing their physical resistance to a very low level and very probably lessening the likelihood of the operation being a success. Negative fears can break down the body's resistance. The dreadful power of negative auto-suggestion can bring on psychosomatic illness and conditions that would probably never exist if it were not for this. On the same level, thinking of pain can make life an even greater hell for a patient lying in bed waiting to be prepared for the operating theatre. Positive thoughts of absolute success of the operation, of the pleasant convalescent times ahead, the final removal of a shadow that has perhaps hovered over the patient for a long time, can work wonders in keeping normal breathing under control, the pulse steady and the mind calm, with the result that the body is already well armed, equipped with a built-in resistance to what lies ahead. Successful operations are performed on positive-minded patients all over the world. In all cases where there is every prospect of complete recovery it is the positive-minded patient who stands the best chance of winning through.

Lots of negative men and women of all ages just love talking about operations, hospitalisation, doctor's surgeries, potions, pills and placebos. They are never better than when they are ill, mostly from imagined complaints. Such folk gain the only attention they will ever get from friends and family by reciting, on a regular, compulsive basis, an endless list of complaints that they hope will draw attention to themselves. Almost inevitably the only attention they *do* get is from others equally determined never to be well.

Case 3: Passing a driving test

Undoubtedly youngsters of both sexes seem capable of passing a driving test first go, whereas their elders, parents, uncles, aunts and so on, tend to have to have two, three or even four tests before finally they can remove their L plates in triumph. This is mainly because the younger, probably teenage, mind is uncluttered with the normal responsibilities of adulthood, its troubles and trials and tribulations in the complex world of today. Youth is far more carefree, lacking in responsibilities and is, therefore, more able quickly to absorb knowledge and information. The young male mind regards a car as a social asset – something with which to 'attract the girls' – so the sooner he is legally able to sit behind a driving wheel so much the better! Girls are equally as eager to pass a driving test as soon as possible as they need the freedom it gives them. With those ambitions and compulsions in mind it is no wonder they *do* succeed, so often, in passing a test the very first time. The will to win is there from the very first moment that they sit in a car next to an instructor. The young male and female minds are already positively protected against failure and positively influenced by thoughts of instant success.

The adult mind, on the other hand, can probably entertain negative fears of what *might* happen when they are on the road. '*Suppose I run over a cat or a dog? Suppose I knock someone down? Suppose I have to be breathalysed? Suppose I forget something in the Highway Code? Suppose I crash? Suppose someone crashes into me?*' And all those thoughts are in the mind during driving instruction and often during the test itself. But most, if not all, negative thoughts such as these are caused by the fact that there is the driving instructor in the passenger seat watching every movement. Most adult drivers, having passed the test, sigh with relief that at last they are alone; there is no one suddenly to put their hand on the steering wheel, to jam on the dual-control brakes or to whistle through their teeth in sudden fear. At last they are gloriously alone.

Many driving instructors tend to put their pupils into a negative state of mind and this must, at all costs, be fought off with determination by the pupil driver. The tension that exists when the pupil steps into the car with the instructor or examiner must be positively dispelled by the pupil before their hands are on the steering-wheel and they have turned the key in the ignition.

Many examiners, like the schoolteachers of earlier years, have a capacity to induce in the pupil feelings of inadequacy merely because they are in a position to fail the examinee. Because of this momentary position of authority over the learner driver, they have it in their power to make their victim a mass of nerves, waiting tensely for the next instruction to turn left or right, do an emergency stop or a three point turn. When it comes to questions on the Highway Code the would-be driver suffers a mental block, a temporary blackout that can cause all the carefully learnt answers to melt away into thin air when the vital probings are under way.

But all this, to the adequate pupil undergoing the test, is a battle of wills between themselves and the examiner. Positive thinkers, an hour or so before the test, have conditioned themselves to refuse to be a bundle of nerves; to dismiss all ideas that the examiner is a monster out to fail them at the slightest excuse. They know the Highway Code inside-out and no one is going to fog their powers of recall through sheer nerves or feelings of inferiority. They have learnt, by now, all the rudiments of driving. They know all about clutch-control on a hill. They know their mirror drill, hand signals, they know instinctively, now, which pedal to use when. Why should the examiner sitting in the passenger seat have the power to make them forget all these things they have learnt so well after many hours of driving tuition? Positive thinkers tell themselves they will pass the moment they step through the doors of the driving school for the test. They do not regard the examiner with apprehension the moment they set eyes on him when their name is called out. They do not follow him or her with fear and trembling to the car. They do not fasten their safety-belt, filled with foreboding. They read the number plate of the car ahead with clear eyes and in a clear voice. They turn the ignition key in the lock with confidence as they hear the engine purr into action. They adjust the mirror with professional pride and accuracy before putting the gear into first and driving off with the usual glances all around.

All actions are positive, powerful and purposeful. The picture of ultimate success they hold in their mind throughout the test, obeying the examiner's instructions as if it was they, themselves driving alone and giving themselves the instructions. 'I am going to pass' they keep telling themselves as, with their eyes on the road and their ears tuned to the examiner's orders, they drive smoothly and happily round the test course. 'How nice it will be', positive thinkers muse, 'when I will be able to drive my own car without those inhibiting L plates front and rear.' And so it *will* be. The positive thinkers answer the Highway Code questions with aplomb. They drive better than at any time during their driving instruction. Back at the test HQ they are home and dry. The longed-for pass is in their hands. Look at every driver on the road every day of every week of every month of every year. They are all *positive thinkers*, sure of themselves and with the will to win. You *can* be one of them!

Case 4: Addressing an audience

It is the first time ever you have been asked to speak to, or to lecture to an audience, either in the local church hall, at a wedding reception, at a political meeting or whatever. You are by no means a trained public speaker but this is something you have been asked to do as a favour or maybe for cash on your first engagement as a professional speaker. Probably you make copious notes for your address, pace up and down your living room declaiming to thin air as you rehearse your speech, memorising your lines as you go. Or you are more practical and make headings, in large block capitals, for the various stages of your talk, the headings to be used to remind you of what you have to say next.

The positive thinker will use that method rather than write an entire rigmarole of words and phrases as the headlines alone should serve to recall the substance of each idea to follow and to be impressed upon the audience. The positive speaker with personality and the power of projection will dismiss, instantly, any idea of reading his address from a written script. Nothing so bores an audience as a speaker obviously just reading from a script, without expression or feeling or gesture or intonation or change of pace. Positive thinkers dismiss the thought of forgetting their lines. They decide to rely on those all-important headlines and when they reach each one of them they recall instantly the substance of the headlines and enlarge on them, with a well-modulated voice, full of expression, adding witty and apt phrases to make them even more interesting. Not having to peer down at notes all of the time, the speakers can allow themselves to look directly at the audience, making them seem in closer contact with them and, at the same time, using their hands to animate and stress important points.

They can change facial expressions to fit the mood of their words for they do not have to hold a fixed and firm look as they read from a continuous script. Positive thinkers do not allow frogs which are born of nerves and stage-fright to get in their throats. They do not mumble and bumble so that only unintelligible sounds come from their lips. They speak in an articulate manner, placing emphasis where it is needed, adding tone and colour to their voice and injecting humour where suitable and possible. In this positive manner they become, not merely a speaker or a lecturer but an actor able to catch and to hold the audience's rapt attention.

These techniques can and should also apply to the after-dinner speaker who is engaged to address a satiated and drink-filled room of diners. Their speech should appear to be spontaneous as befits the occasion. Tension in the nerve-wracked speaker or lecturer makes itself painfully apparent in their hesitancy and frequent throat-clearing coughs, as they indulge in embarrassing attempts at jokey humour. Positive-minded speakers hold audience from start to finish and, if question-time follows, their personality still dominates the scene. Such assurance takes practice, but even on the occasion of your first public speech, if you approach it positively, you should actually enjoy it, regarding it as good experience for the many engagements to follow.

In all of these four cases tension is often caused by anxiety over the possibility of pain or the fear of failure when success is, naturally, desired. It is a 'Will it or will it not?' 'Will I or will I not?' situation. A conflict between adequacy and possible inadequacy. Inferiority or superiority. Negative or positive. Minus or plus. Not all of us can be positive all of the time. *But many can be negative all of the time.* As suggested in Chapter One, negativity is born of past unfortunate experiences whereas positivity depends upon our dismissal of all our yesterdays and their negative influences. The present visit to the dentist is overshadowed by our first, childhood encounter with a dentist. The present impending operation in hospital is over-shadowed by that tonsil operation in childhood. The present failure of the driving test is brought about by failure in school exams. The present challenge at public speaking or any sort of confrontation with an audience is influenced by a regrettable failure at speech-making at a school bazaar or some such function.

The old recalled tensions build up within us. The fear of pain is magnified and pushed out of focus. The dread of examinations is clouded over by past failures and mixing socially with success is tempered by past embarrassments and gaffes.

Probably if we did not have the power of recall we would never fear anything and always have an everlasting confidence that would allow us to win through at almost everything. But the notion 'Forewarned is forearmed' is vital to self-preservation when danger threatens. So it seems we must accept this ever-present subconscious remembrance of what happened yesterday in order to warn us of unwise moves that might be made today. We see now, however, that too much reflection on what happened in the past can be injurious to present moves which might influence the future. Common sense must prevail every time in weighing up the negative against the positive and this is where the power of positive thinking is put to the acid test in regard to selectivity.

We do not wish to put ourselves in the same position as Job of biblical times who announced dolefully: 'That which I most feared has come upon me!'

16

THOUGHT POWER CAN CREATE YOUR PHILOSOPHY

As we think, so, undoubtedly, we *are*. And what we *are* reflects our philosophy of life.

Philosophy is a knowledge of existence. An attitude towards it. An optimism or a pessimism. An acceptance of the inevitable or a determination to change what seems to be inevitable and to shape and form life in the way we wish it to be for us. A strong desire to form a positive conception of life.

Our personal philosophy determines what we do with our life. And that, of course, is entirely dependent upon how we *think*. It reflects our spiritual values; our way with power and possessions. We all have a philosophy towards life even if it is not always obvious either to ourselves or those around us. Naturally this sense of how we wish to run our lives arises from early days, parenting, environment, what we learn at school and, later, our happy and unhappy experiences in life.

Very often a career reflects a philosophy in life. The career is chosen and followed either because our individual thought power makes a particular career inevitable, or the career shapes and forms and develops our latent and unrealised attitude towards life. And so our thought power is enhanced and strengthened as the years go by.

Thoughts take a certain direction in life. We are here concentrating on the positive thoughts that determine the philosophies deep within the individual. In order to demonstrate the link between philosophy and a chosen or intended career, here are a few examples of those links. Possibly you may recognise yourself among them.

Philosophy	Career
The sinner should be punished. The malefactor must be caught.	Police officer Lawyer Magistrate Judge
The sick should be healed. Suffering must be allayed.	Doctor Nurse Surgeon
God is Life. Humanity must be saved from itself. Life hereafter is the goal of all earthly endeavour.	Priest Missionary Evangelist
Mental and emotional life control the physical. The sick in life must be healed of aberrations.	Psychologist Psychiatrist Faith healer
Money makes money. High pressure wins. Morals and conscience do not matter. Exploitation means expectation.	Investor Business tycoon Industrialist Magnate Con-man
Life is creative. Expression through the arts reflects life itself. Everything has life, colour, vibrations, movement and rhythm.	Artist Writer Composer Designer

This does not mean that all investors, business tycoons, industrialists and magnates followed their chosen careers because they believed in these somewhat ruthless and, in some cases, negative philosophies!

But what if you are not working in one of these career areas, does that mean you do not have a philosophy in life? Obviously, it does not. Sometimes our philosophy shows up more clearly in out-of-work activities, the kind of voluntary organisations and societies we belong to, the belief we follow, the way we live our lives.

Your strength may be that others turn to you for support and guidance and people regard you as a force for good in the community. Perhaps you carry a donor card or give blood regularly – both are signs that you are a caring person. These things are all the result of a positive philosophy in life. They may seem to be rather small unimportant things to you, but they are all born of positive, kindly thinking.

You may well indulge yourself in the philosophy of positivism which sounds something like this:

> 'I was born without asking to be born, I was put into the world without my permission. Well, OK! So the world is mine. It asked for me. Now it's got me. It's got to like me, accept me, my ideas, my thoughts, my philosophy. The world now owes me a living. A good one, at that. I'm going to get it. I know what I want and I will get to know all those people who will help me to get what I want, but in the nicest possible way, of course. No taking advantage of anyone on the way. No con-tricks.'

Is that *you*, do you think?

On the other hand, hopefully you do not indulge in the philosophy of negativism, which sounds something like this:

> 'The dirtiest trick my parents ever played on me was having me! There are thousands, millions, just like me who wish they had never been born. What chance have I of ever making a success of my life? The world doesn't have to keep me if it doesn't want to. I'm of no importance. Maybe I am to my parents. But that's just by the way. No one likes me. I'm a nonentity. No one is ever likely to want to help me. I will never get what I want.'

Many people have to suffer a little before they gain the correct outlook on life. But sometimes suffering spurs people on to find a better life. The positive mind shines through and a new life is formed from past, unfortunate mistakes and experiences. The complacent, ever-happy, ever-successful person is more than likely to develop a selfish outlook, even to regard those less lucky with a certain sort of contempt. Bad luck at times can be a blessing as far as the development of positive thought and a positive philosophy is concerned.

Under duress many of us can develop into far better, positive-minded individuals. We can even accomplish great things. Oscar Wilde wrote 'The Ballad of Reading Gaol' while in prison. Damon Runyon wrote the best of his short stories while in gaol. Their aim was to vindicate themselves. They did, although the unsophisticated generation of Oscar Wilde's days rejected him in the end.

But this is *today*. Today frustration can be defeated. You need no longer look upon philosophers as members of some select society, or day-dreamers. You can recognise them all as people who have learned to like life, who make people like *them*. And you can join them so easily, so quickly, by creating your own positive philosophy and outlook born of positive thought.

To that end, the next chapter will provide you with a daily formula for positive thinking which, applied to yourself upon waking each morning, will shape and form your personal philosophy that will carry you successfully through the day.

17

YOUR FORMULA FOR HAVING A GOOD DAY

When you get up each morning set the positive theme of your day by forgetting any negative things that happened yesterday that gave rise to problems. Dismiss all that was of a negative nature. Learn off by heart the following formula for a good day and repeat it to yourself while getting ready to face your day.

Formula for having a good day

I will have a strong desire to overcome all opposition.

I will make the most of all today has to offer.

I will enjoy every moment of today.

I will not worry over what I have not.

I will make the most of what I have.

I will be content with this day and be grateful for it.

I will not hanker after what I cannot obtain.

I will add more love and compassion for others today.

I will try to understand others more today.

I will try to understand myself even more.

I will attempt to increase my mental awareness.

During your good day you will not accept negative suggestions projected to you by others but will counter them by your own positive thought projections. You will neither encourage nor cultivate a negative attitude towards yourself because of unwanted and unfair criticism aimed at you. You will not, in short, allow your mind to get into such a receptive state that it is open to negative thoughts.

Every day the air is constantly filled with thought waves aimed at you for good or for bad. These are attitudes that make themselves felt by the expression in people's eyes when they look at you, by the sound of their voices when they speak to you, by the little things they do to please or to annoy you. Their negative attitudes towards you can be countered in many subtle ways: taking them off their guard, diminishing their unpleasant attempts to upset you, disarming them by making them see how small minded is their sarcasm and cynicism.

Study the following table of reverse attitudes. Apply them during your day and see how they confuse and confound those who deliberately set themselves up in opposition to you.

Table of reverse attitudes

If they are:	You should be:
Belligerent	Gently firm
Aggressive	Reasonable
Bombastic	Really cool!
Demanding	Tolerant
Pushy	Gently persuasive
Physically violent	Strongly in command
Unreasonable	Understanding
Overbearing	Gently amused

Turning the other cheek? Not really. Just disarming them, that's all. An amused flicker in your eye will quickly baffle an irate person. A clever response will tongue-tie the verbal attacker. A show of calmness will conquer the belligerent, aggressive, bombastic personality.

There is a positive, powerful mental laser beam from your brain that will explode any incoming negative thought-missile from a protagonist – a sort of Star Wars attack on their sensibilities!

Every one of your days can be a battle of wits between you and those with whom you come into contact.

Being aggressive is not being positive—
the defensive. Being aggressive causes co
rarely has a positive conclusion. Being calm
mindedness calculated to upset and to confuse an
person in the long run. The adrenalin may well rise
verbal or physical strife, but it is positivism that quells
it down to a sane and a sensible level that quickly overc
serious developments.

Your 'Formula for having a good day', plus the 'Table of rev
attitudes', taken to heart and learnt with interest and enthusiasm
will help you to counter any negative assault upon your mind that
may occur in your daily routine. It can also constructively assist the
woman or man who does not go out to work but who is faced with
the often soul-destroying domestic chores of looking after the home:
tending to the children, fighting boredom, facing up to the strain of
supermarket shopping, visits by unwelcome and boring neighbours,
fetching offspring back from a shouting, screaming school play-
ground at tea time.

Positive thinking works in all areas of life. We must all cultivate it
and use it to good purpose in our own particular struggle against
day-to-day trials and tribulations.

...e lack of confidence in what we are
doing. Tensi.... ...g-machine of the ability to act upon
one thought at a time, thereby giving rise to a confusion of thoughts
and ideas.

Tension manifests itself in trembling, excitement, nervousness,
hesitation, irritation, depression, nausea – all of which adds up to an
unenviable nervous state.

Other reasons for tension overcoming the normal process of
positive thinking are lack of sleep, eating and drinking to excess or
not eating enough, smoking too much, poor bodily elimination, a
deficiency of vitamins, minerals or protein, poor blood circulation,
unresolved anxieties, unrelieved repressions, fixed inhibitions, confused thinking of a negative nature, social, industrial or domestic
stress, too little time in which to do too much, too little to do in too
much time. Quite a list!

Such adverse conditions and influences – imagined or actual –
plus curtailment of personal freedom of thought and action, self-
expression and creative outlets, over-stimulate the thinking
processes and paralyse the nervous system.

Glandular fluids such as adrenalin, sex hormones and thyroxine
are manufactured in the body. When these are circulating in the
bloodstream with no satisfactory outlet the brain becomes thrown
out of gear, nerves are 'torn to shreds', the body and the mind reel
under the sense of conflict and eventually 'go to pieces'.

Tension has attacked.

Positive thinking has a hard task trying to battle forward as
confused negative thoughts take over.

Nevertheless, and conversely, too much rest and relaxation and
too much pleasure, can have the same effects, because the brain
becomes too inactive.

Success can also cause tension; when a peak has been reached it is difficult but important to your self-respect to maintain it. Comedians worry about their performances, how to maintain the same level expected of them by their audiences. Successful bosses in commerce must keep the pace going so that profits do not drop, manufacturers must maintain a steady flow of production to satisfy their market and so on.

Tension can be contagious. Like fear, it spreads. People become aware of the tensed-up personality, become nervous and tensed-up themselves. Mass hysteria and mob rule manifesting themselves in protests, demonstrations, attacks on the public and the police are all results of tension magnified to its uttermost degree.

Tension must have an escape route and finds it in fright and escape. Escape from reality. Escape from fact. Flight from action and responsibility.

You know tension is attacking when:

small things upset you unreasonably;

sleep at night fails to refresh you;

relaxation fails to help you;

you worry away from your job as well as at it;

you develop a nervous spasm or 'tic';

your fingers twitch and turn in agitation, hands are restless;

your teeth are clenched, your jaw is tightened.

Unpleasant symptoms to say the least.

Might you be suffering from tension? Ask yourself if:

daily, well-accustomed noises annoy you more than ever;

lights dazzle and irritate your eyes, sunlight proves painful;

conversation sometimes becomes confused and erratic;

your appetite is far from normal;

your daily routine seems onerous, boring, exhausting?

If tension persists, from day to day, and you can find no real cause for it, and positive thinking about the matter fails to bring about much improvement, try eating better to feed your jangled nerve ends. Take more vitamins. Make yourself ease up, relax, flop out; clear your mind; sleep longer. Talk to someone occasionally. Take more exercise in the fresh air. Escape to the country for a while; take in some sun.

As far as your diet is concerned, eat eggs, drink a mixture of lemon, honey and cider vinegar. Have wholemeal bread, fresh fruit and vegetables. Cut out white bread, white flour, cakes and pastries.

And another great thing is to *laugh more*!

Laughter:

exercises the heart, lungs, stomach, liver, diaphragm;

clears the bronchial tubes and nose;

washes out the eyes, cleanses the tear ducts;

drains blood from the brain, sends more oxygen to the brain.

So there is a lot of easing of tension in a good joke, a hearty laugh, even in a giggle or two!

Consider the following psychosomatic symptoms of ill-health which can be brought on by a negative tension state:

Negative tension state	Psychosomatic symptoms
Confused thoughts and indecision	Giddiness, sense of imbalance
Frustration and inhibition	Pains in the back, lumbago
Secret feelings of guilt	Rashes, skin eruptions
Emotional upsets	Mucous colitis
Repressed sex life	Impotence, frigidity
Over-anxiety, persecution complex	Insomnia; nightmares, if sleeping
Sense of inadequacy	Procrastination, hesitation
Repressing self-expression	Sore throat, palpitations
Suppression of emotional outlets	Heart troubles, breathing problems

This is a menacing list of negative-minded attitudes affecting the body and producing symptoms that have their origin in the mind but which could develop into actual physical conditions themselves if not checked in time.

But just think how positive thinking can cure all that nonsense. Why be an introvert when you can be an extrovert? Why think 'in' rather than 'out'?

We will move on, now, to a few examples of the lesser tensions suffered by the average man and woman, some of them brought on by compulsive behaviour and anxiety complexes; easily curable and removable by positive thinking, but which, if left unchecked, could eventually lead to high-tension states of mind.

A bachelor writes:

I can never go to bed at night in my flat without switching off all lights, unplugging the television, turning off all gas taps, locking all doors and windows. All very sensible, of course. But a few moments after I have got into bed I start asking myself: 'Did I switch off the telly? Did I really turn off the gas taps? Is the front door safely locked against intruders?' And so on. I have to get up out of bed, do all the rounds all over again, saying to myself 'Gas off, taps off, plugs out, switches off, door locked', touching each switch and lock and tap as I do it. Back to bed again. Perhaps a brief period of sleep and then I am at it again! Tension mounts up inside me as I feel sure I did *not*, after all, turn off the gas taps. Perhaps I failed to put the latch on the door after all, as well as locking it up? So, out of bed once again. Once again I do the rounds. Then, at last, I can fall off to sleep. Each morning when I wake, of course, everything *has* been turned off, switched off, locked up and latched. But I know that that every night, before I can drop off to sleep again, the same tension state will rise in me and I will have to go over just the same compulsive routine as ever.

Positive thinking suggests:

You go to bed each night without any concrete evidence that you have, in fact, switched off all lights, unplugged the television, turned off all gas taps, locked all doors and windows. All you do is to switch off and turn off and lock up and unplug, every time saying 'Gas off, lights off' and so on, until the ritual is completed. By the time you get to bed, you no longer trust the sound of your own voice, having repeated those mystic incantations out loud. Your anxiety complex begins to take over and the tension caused brings on the compulsion to get out of bed and go over the same routine all over again. Doubtless you apply this mistrust of yourself and your actions to things you do during the day at work as well. But the main concern is that you cure yourself of this habit *at bedtime* so that you can go to sleep as soon as possible.

In order to allow positive thinking to replace negative thinking over this matter, make a list of items to be checked, one after the other in a single column on a piece of notepaper. Lights, door, gas, television, plugs and so on. As you switch off, unplug, turn off, lock up, make a firm *tick* opposite the item in the column of 'duties' you are performing. Each task accomplished will merit a large tick next to the appropriate word. Take the piece of notepaper to bed, place it on the bedside table, and, before turning out the light, read down the list noting the fact there is a tick next to each item. Common sense will convince you that you would not have put a tick next to each item if, in fact, you had *not* attended to each task consciously and with full awareness. Turn the lights off and go to sleep with the full evidence of your duties duly performed registered on the sheet of notepaper. On the following night put a tick next to last night's tick and repeat this on successive nights until you have a long line of positive ticks right across the paper, giving evidence of your positive, conscious moves each night at bedtime. Do *not*, however, ever mistrust the fact that any one of the ticks on the paper on any night has been put there unconsciously by you, or you will find yourself jumping out of bed all over again in order to convince yourself that a tick *does*, in fact, mean you *have* switched off, unplugged, locked up and so forth.

Do this for as many nights as you deem necessary until finally you see the utter futility of not trusting your bedtime actions. Then you will be able to go to bed and to sleep every single night with no trouble just like everyone else.

A husband writes:

I am 40 years of age and have been married for 10 years now. At my age I am beginning to worry over the fact that I seem to be losing my sexual power – becoming impotent, no less. Lots of my men friends tell me they entertain the same thoughts because, well, the sex books *do* say that, even from the age of 20, a male's sexual prowess does start slowly to diminish. Thoughts of this sort are beginning to cause great tension between my wife and me and our usual routine of a Saturday night sex session is now failing dismally and I just do not seem to be able to act the part any more. You know what I mean, I feel sure! So my wife variously accuses me of hankering after women if not actually having another woman unbeknown to her. I tell her it's not that; it's just that I'm losing my sex power and she must accept that fact. She is only 30 and, naturally, far from frigid. I am so afraid I am going to lose her to some other man who is not growing impotent as I appear to be. The tensions between me and my wife are growing out of all proportion and I am feeling quite desperate about the whole thing.

Positive thinking suggests:

There is absolutely no reason why any man, given average good physical and mental health, should become impotent at the age of 40, 50, 60 or, in fact, even 70. It is obvious that you are tensed-up because of what your misinformed male friends tell you and because of your wife's veiled suggestions and suspicions and evident dissatisfaction at your prowess which appears to be failing. It is all a matter of the most vicious suggestions from others and negative auto-suggestion from yourself. You say later in your very long letter that your doctor has told you more than once that it is 'all in your mind' and that sexual desire and the sexual impulse starts in the mind. How true, of course, but it appears he has not taken the trouble to tell you exactly how the sexual mechanism works. Instead, as you state, he has given you tranquillisers that appear to have slowed you down further. If you tell yourself you *are* impotent, you will *be* impotent, incapable of gaining an erection which is, of course, absolutely necessary for sexual intercourse to take place.

So, put your positive thinking cap on right now and learn and absorb the following true and well-proven facts. Sexual arousal does, most certainly, begin in the mind, as your doctor has said. Erection is the result of psychic impressions, not merely overexcited sex glands. Testicular hormones reach the brain so that erotic thoughts quickly gather. Thoughts of past sexual experiences are aroused, thoughts of possible present and immediate sexual joy further excites, and these erotic images transmit themselves, through the nervous system which is connected with the penis. This brings about tremendous mental and physical stimulation, the result of which is the erection. This is the biological way of working things out so that penetration of the female can take place.

It becomes obvious, then, that a successful male erection is precipitated by positive thoughts of success and that failure to gain an erection is caused by tensed-up, negative thoughts of failure. This sense of ultimate failure is, naturally, brought about by outside suggestion of failure to perform, which can include scorn and adverse criticism from your wife, from other men who seek to deflate you in more ways than one and by auto-suggestion on your part that, at the age of 40, you are becoming impotent.

If you *think* you will fail you *will* fail, because the messages being sent down from your brain are negative convictions of failure and your body will, therefore, react accordingly. Abject failure on one occasion remains in the mind and is resurrected against at a second attempt. It will happen again, you tell yourself. And it *will* and it *does*! If a man with a scornful, cruelly critical wife has intercourse with another woman, invariably he will be successful, for the scorn and the criticism will not be there. Many, many women make their men functionally impotent because they tell them they are 'useless in bed'. Only by using the knowledge you have just gained by this explanation of the workings of the sexual impulse, combined with a determination to overcome your negative thoughts of impotence and the frustrated gibes from your partner, will you gain full potency again. Until ill-health or genuine old age take over you can still be the masculine male.

A housewife writes:

My husband earns an excellent salary as a managing director. Our son is grown-up and away from home, as is our daughter. Both have good jobs and we see them only on rare occasions as our son is in New York and our daughter in Australia. We have a lovely home in Gloucestershire, complete with a large garden. I am 50 and my husband is five years older. We have a daily help and a live-in cook. You would think I would be very happy indeed. But I am not. Nearly every day, after my husband has driven off to the neighbouring town for his working day, I start being assailed by unpleasant, tensed-up thoughts. Suppose he has an accident going to his office, or on his way back? Supposing our son is taken ill thousands of miles away in New York? What would happen to our daughter in Australia if she was injured, attacked by some man or got into any sort of trouble? Is it possible, could it be possible, that my husband's firm could suddenly collapse, go bankrupt or something awful like that? How could we manage to keep on this house? Where would we go? Thoughts like that simply crowd in on me time after time. It's been like this for nearly a year now. Even our Spanish holiday this year didn't dispel the tension which enveloped me once again upon our return as life resumed its normal routine.

Positive thinking suggests:

Long days of loneliness, apart from the presence of your daily help and cook, spent in your large house and garden are beginning to prey upon you. You have learnt that money and possessions and power do not, of necessity, make for happiness. What you lack in life is some creative, productive outlet. You say you have your own car, and that the neighbouring town is only a matter of a few miles away. Negative thoughts of a nebulous nature crowd in on you and make you tense because of their implications of tragedy and dire distress. Thinking positively would get you out of the house for several days a week to join a club, a local art centre or a voluntary service organisation for children or old people. Positive thought on your part would make you think of yourself as someone other than a dutiful (not to mention well-off and idle) wife and you would become a person in your own right, useful to others apart from your husband. Venturing out and leaving the house to look after itself would do you the world of good. It would save you from these introspective, negative tension-creating thoughts and imaginings. Do all those things and you will see a marked difference in next to no time.

An art student writes:

I am a girl of 18. I have attended art school in London for two years and am now faced with important exams which I will have to sit in a few weeks' time. I am hoping to gain a degree in Art and Graphics which will include fashion designing. As the days of the exam draw nearer I find I am getting tense. Tense about whether I shall remember all I have learnt, about computer graphics, various type-faces used in print, and the materials and textiles in fashion design. I know I have the knowledge. I have studied hard and with great enthusiasm for I know there is a good future in those fields if I get my degree. I fear my mind will go a complete blank when I am faced with the exam papers. I also have to carry out practical creative and design work. If I am tense now what on earth will I feel like on the actual days of the exams?

Positive thinking suggests:

The actor or actress rehearsing a part in a play feels a build-up of nervous tension from the first read-through of the script through rehearsals to the dress rehearsal. And also, of course, stagefright before going on stage on the first night. But, on stage, with the spotlights on, the hushed audience out there waiting with expectancy, the stagefright or nervous tension disappears and the actor or actress gives a great performance. Like an actress, you know your lines to perfection. You know the play inside out. All your cues. All your entrances and exits. But naturally you are tense with nervousness and expectation. Some actors and actresses are physically sick before going on stage for a performance. They get rid, in this physical way, all of their doubts and nervous tension and stagefright. So purged, they make a successful entrance and give a good performance.

You, also, can purge yourself of your nervous tension as you wait to take your seat in the examination hall, Not by being sick, but by forcibly and mentally purging yourself of all negative tension-thoughts that have been building up over the weeks leading up to exam day. You know you know your stuff backwards, as the actress knows the play's lines backwards. On the night before the exams clear your mind of all tension. Forget about trying to remember what you will have to do. Have a good night's rest. Awake refreshed, knowing that all you have learnt is still there. There will be *no* mental blackouts. Your subconscious mind will come up with all the answers to all the questions, your fingers will create all the models you will be required to design because your subconscious mind has it all there waiting for you, in a cool, calm state of positive-mindedness, to bring it all to the surface.

Those four cases illustrate simple situations that can give rise to nervous tension, the effects being to negate positive thinking and to throw it completely out of action. It becomes obvious, then, that greater crises can produce far greater and longer-lasting tensions with the psychosomatic results listed earlier on in this chapter.

Tension occurs when stress gets stretched to its uttermost limits. While stress will cause anxiety, sudden feelings of inadequacy and confused thinking, the onset of stress attacks the body via your mental attitudes, and this inevitably brings on the tension conditions of a mind-body relationship that is completely out of touch with rationality.

Tension-states can be conquered by going out, so to speak, and fighting the cause. The inadequate personality fails to discover or to acknowledge the root of the problem. There is no fight to eradicate the cause and the tension persists, growing worse as the hours go by.

Quite a lot of tension is caused by an overwrought imagination which builds mental mountains out of imaginary molehills. What someone said, what suddenly happened, what small fear lurks in the background of the mind, what negative suggestion has suddenly been promoted in the mind by an outside influence, grows out of all proportion in the imagination of the victim. Going out to meet the threat, analysing it, breaking it down to commonsense levels and proportions constitutes the positive attack. Accepting it, giving way to the imagined or actual threat is the negative attitude. Forewarned is forearmed.

19

THE POSITIVE VALUE OF
MEANING SOMETHING
TO SOMEONE

Living *for* someone as well as living *with* someone, married or otherwise, is a great boost to morale and a state of existence that demands a positive state of mind.

From the very moment we are born we belong to someone and therefore we mean something to someone, our parents predominantly and relatives on either side almost equally so. When we grow up and finally leave home it is often for the purpose of belonging to someone else and therefore meaning something *to* someone else. In today's world this can mean inside or outside the married state. A secretary means something to her boss, but she also means something completely different to her partner. At some time she may mean something to her own child or children.

Self-confessed 'loners' proudly state that solitude is great. Withdrawal from the social scene makes them 'interesting' to onlookers. Some may even dub them intellectuals, for they say little, but it is believed they think a lot. Think a lot they undoubtedly do, but mainly about *themselves*. Very often they become egotists, people who consider themselves above all others and who are incapable of thinking of others in their mean and narrow existence. They feel they know more, see more and can do more than other people. Invariably, they are introverts as well.

Loners often becomes eccentrics and this, though they probably do not realise it is an unconscious attempt to draw others to them. The effect is usually the opposite. Eccentrics embarrass others. They are given a wide berth, unless, of course, their eccentricity is part of their personality – they are unconscious eccentrics. Nature has made them so and they would not be nearly so interesting if they consciously tried to change their ways. Unconscious eccentrics can be very endearing people – it is the conscious eccentric we must beware of: the person who affects a pose in an effort to seem different from the 'ordinary' people to whom they feel mentally superior.

The only people such characters mean anything to are themselves, without a doubt. And the same can apply to loners who maybe fear contact with people – a fear created out of years of thinking negatively about people and situations. Possessing a strong sense of inadequacy they withdraw from social contacts, thereby making themselves sufficient unto themselves alone, and gladly renouncing any need to mean anything to anyone. It then follows that their life just has to be based on a negative-thought input.

It is well nigh impossible to live happily for oneself alone. No love in life but oneself. No children of one's own to watch grow and develop. No sound career to follow. No contribution to make to the world. No flowers at the funeral.

Compare this to the fellow or the girl with positive thoughts of belonging to loving parents and meaning a great deal to them. And then leaving home and becoming useful to some employer, and to oneself as well, in a lucrative career. Then the falling-in-love process, and realising that devotion to one's parents has now changed and developed to include someone else outside the family circle. There is now someone else in life to care for and that someone reciprocates the feeling.

Most loners and conscious eccentrics have a grievance against life. That is their justification for being alive. They don't really want to be dead for that would rob them of their negative attitudes towards life. They are martyrs to their own mental outlook. However, many will argue that their eccentricity is born of genius and there have indeed been many eccentric people in the past who have made their mark in history, but again these are the unconscious eccentrics who may have been so singleminded in the pursuit of excellence in their chosen or predetermined field that they had no time or thought for the conventional way of living. But genius is a very rare thing and is not a term that can be applied to many of us.

Having a capacity for caring for someone else in life is a special kind of genius in its own right, for it takes one out of oneself and makes one aware of others: their lives, their feelings and emotions, their cares and worries and anxieties. And this imparts the urge to be of help and assistance – a very positive thought! In encouraging this it closely involves us in the life of another person. In such a close and caring situation there can be little room for negative thinking.

The difference between a loner or an eccentric is a matter of the individual's own approach. As an individual you can find a niche in society, a place in commerce. Best of all – a place in someone's heart.

With a pleasant, happy, outgoing, extrovert personality exemplifying positive thoughts and attitudes towards others you can at once begin to mean something, not only to one person, but to many. To your friends in your social life. Your workmates or office colleagues. Your husband, wife or lover.

They all *want* you. And there is nothing better than being wanted. Ask yourself:

Who is kept happy and alert and alive by you?

Who looks to you for support and inspiration?

Who lives for you – and you alone?

If there is only *one person* then that is enough. Enough to show that you are sending out beams of positive thought that you honestly and truly *care*.

The rewards can be great.

20

A STRONG CHARACTER IS THE
RESULT OF POSITIVE THOUGHT

The devious character rarely thinks in a positive manner. If he does it is usually to plan something of a negative nature.

The person who thinks in a positive manner, all of the time, cannot help but develop and demonstrate a sound, strong character. It becomes second nature.

Once character has been formed very little can change its basic qualities. But suffering, poverty, deprivation and bereavement can make severe dents in it that can take away the positive elements and replace them with negative ones. The God-fearing and God-loving person can lose faith in the event of tragedy as in the death of a loved one. When tragic, sad or unfortunate incidents happen in life the believer can say, 'Why me?' and faith and belief, previously strong character points, can go for ever.

A strong will can be severely undermined by abject disappointment caused by failing to achieve success in a particular project. The appalling and criminal act of murder can so shake a mild, caring character that negative thought takes over and turns a gentle person into one who can think of nothing but revenge. Trouble of any sort can often so unbalance a steady and reliable character that it becomes completely shaken out of gear and the entire attitude towards life changes.

However, as can be shown by graphology, which is the art of reading character in handwriting, dominant characteristics remain for ever and cannot entirely be removed under any circumstances. The positive thinker, in times of trouble, struggles to retain these dominant characteristics and does not allow them to be lost in a flurry of self-inflicted negative blows.

Character illustrates, to a great extent, your personal outlook on life and your attitude towards your fellow-beings. If you do not know the difference between good and bad you have an amoral character, but if you can tell right from wrong then you are a moral person. If you are given to adventurous and often risky sexual habits your character is immoral.

It is true that:

Character traits that live up to social standards are good.

Character traits that go against ethics and morals are bad.

The bad character comes into conflict with society.

The good character adds to the social scene in every way.

And, quite obviously, it is all a question of positive thinking towards life and towards all those with whom you come into contact. Man's main aim is self-preservation, but some criminal types do seem to live, unaccountably, on a knife edge!

If you are one of the many millions of positive, forward thinkers in the civilised world you probably have both moral and physical courage and are able to control your emotions in any crisis, personal or otherwise. You should also possess spiritual courage, for the atheist and the agnostic are at a severe disadvantage in life.

The capacity to be caring and loving, as suggested in the previous chapter, is also a vital contribution to a positive character.

Consider this summation of a good, positive character – and see just how well *you* fit in.

The positive character:

inspires confidence;

does not support class distinction or racism;

is tolerant of others and their failings;

is not amoral or immoral;

is willing to be of assistance to others;

contributes something to society every day;

ultimately contributes to life itself.

Your keynotes of positive character should be resourcefulness, determination, command of all situations, good manners, observance of social standards, direction in life, consideration for others, truthfulness and poise rather than pose.

Don't get the impression those foregoing qualities mean you are a 'goody-goody'. By no means. So-called 'goody-goodies' are usually self-centred, exhibitionist types seeking adulation from others. And most of their good deeds are aimed at improving their own situation and status.

Let us also consider situations that can possibly affect character in a negative manner, situations in which positive thinking and attitudes can be so affected in a negative manner as to *destroy* character.

1 If aims and ambitions in life are too high and impossible to realise, character may well suffer in one who is unable to accept disappointment and to meet it halfway.

2 Inferiority and inadequacy caused by failure may arrest character development, cripple logical emotional outlooks and cause a negative outlook to set in for all time.

3 Abject failure in life may bring about emotional regression to childhood, halting further progress and losing the will to fight back.

Ability and capability have a natural ceiling, a limit to endeavours. By attempting to go beyond this limit you may find disillusionment will set in and reason is destroyed by a strong sense of failure.

Every man and woman has a trace of neuroticism in his or her character make-up. That is the off-beat, off-key strain lurking in the background, waiting to be developed or rejected. This essentially dangerous trait in the character can be sublimated by diverting it into useful, creative, productive and positive channels. Free will is the defensive weapon against neurotic tendencies, and if used in a positive thinking manner can dismiss negative moves of a destructive nature.

People who permit a neurotic outlook to dominate their character in a crisis rarely have the ability to lead. Rather, they become those who are led.

Character, according to Warren's *Dictionary of Psychology*, is 'the moral nature of an individual. A phase of personality comprising the more enduring traits which are of ethical and social significance'.

'Ethical and social significance' is personified by the recognition of good moral behaviour in opposition to amorality and immorality, as already discussed in this chapter. Those 'more enduring traits' are maintained and demonstrated by positive thinking, for positive thinking makes most things possible whereas negative thought destroys.

Character to the individual is like touch to the pianist, technique to the painter, style to the writer. It is that quality that inspires the onlooker and the participant with calm, cool confidence and acceptance of the person who projects this positive quality.

In the next chapter we shall indulge in a ruthless examination of the positive qualities of our own personalities.

21

DO YOU THINK POSITIVELY?

This is not one of those popular newspaper quizzes where you score so many points for good and so many for bad. You must discover or decide for yourself just how you rate when you read the questions put forward here. Only *you* know the correct answers, and, certainly, they merit far more than a pleasing array of score marks! It is a question of being quite ruthless with yourself this time. There is no one else but you, after all, so if you rate rather badly in your estimation who is to know and who is to care but yourself? The great thing is that you will learn about yourself, discover just how adequate or inadequate you are, how positive minded or negative minded you may happen to be.

So here goes . . .

Do I become sarcastic when I lose in an argument?

Do I love self-pity as an indulgence?

Do I easily become influenced by false glamour and surface effects?

Do I think all my ideas are good and no one should challenge them?

Do I blame my age if frustrated in making good progress?

Now have a look at the more positive side.

Do I always know exactly what I want when I set out to get it?

Do I always recognise the motives behind all I do and all I say?

Do I always check facts, or do I take them for granted?

Do I delve into my problems or just skate over them haphazardly?

Do I head straight for my goals and disallow discouragement?

Do I stop others from dominating me?

Do I show willingness to change my views when common sense dictates I should?

Am I really earnest about everything of importance in my life?

Am I generally well in control of my temper in trying circumstances?

Am I generally able to forgive others when they offend me?

Am I always able to complete all tasks I have to perform, big or small?

Am I ready to let pleasure go by the board in favour of hard effort?

Am I able to get others to confide in me?

There should have been all 'yes' answers to *that* list!

People who think negatively are often in the habit of devaluing themselves. They can never graciously accept a compliment and are always commenting on how much more clever so and so is or more beautiful or witty. They are probably much better in all these areas than they think they are but by constantly denying it they come to disbelieve it and never look on the positive side, which would increase their sense of self-esteem. There is no reason why you should not be far better than actually you think you are. So let the world know how good you are. The world will believe you if you are positive about it!

The formula is simple: think tops and you will *be* tops. Think big and you can *be* big. Don't blame yourself for everything that may go wrong. Say when you think you are in the wrong, but do assert yourself strongly and in a positive way when you know you are in the right. People will think well of you if you do. Taking the blame can make others feel stronger than you. Never take the guilt of others on to your own shoulders: you will be made a scapegoat if you do. Never devalue yourself and your own judgments and decisions. Then you will avoid failure in all that you do by not committing the sins of:

omission

neglect

evasion

procrastination

fear to face up to difficulties

fear of failure

overdoing things

over-emphasis

over-anxiety

The negative thinker (which you are *not* by now, we hope) makes people with whom they come into contact think they are a martyr, a yes-man, is impatient, is insecure, unable to make and to keep friends, is inferior, frustrated and inadequate!

You, on the other hand, are the person who never says 'Yes' when you know that 'No' is the proper answer. You never commit the sin of omission by failing to do what you know you have to do. You do not neglect or evade important issues. Certainly, you never procrastinate and you have no fear of facing up to problems. In addition, you have no fear of failure because, as a positive-minded person, you do not permit the word 'failure' to exist in your daily output of words and thoughts. You are not likely to over-do things because you know full well when restraint is desirable and vitally necessary. You don't over-emphasize your points to the edge of anxiety in case they are not getting over.

That sums you up as an individual who neither underestimates nor undervalues yourself.

A positive thinker – no less!

If you find difficulty in thinking positively in a tricky situation, try to be objective about it. Stand away from the problem and try to view it as an outsider would see it. Visualise a positive-minded friend tackling the question and imagine how he or she would deal with it. Often your way forward then seems dazzlingly clear.

Finally, being totally ruthless with yourself, make sure as a *genuine* positive thinker, that you do not give way to:

chronic complaining

self-assertiveness out of proportion to the truth

sarcasm

cynicism

pessimism

aggressiveness

self-centredness

lack of sympathy and understanding

timidity

excessive embarrassment

self-consciousness and feelings of inadequacy

22

EIGHT WAYS TO MAKE YOURSELF A POSITIVE PERSON

Whatever your age may be there is ample opportunity to be positive all of the time, more especially in this computerised, progressive world. For those who are looking forward to being part of the twenty-first century (probably to be the most exciting hundred years of all time), consider the following eight ways in which you can increase your positivity intrinsically through the power of positive thinking above all else, for thought is the dominating influence in your life. It controls your actions and your attitudes, influences those with whom you come into contact every single day of your life.

1 Get as close as you can to the meaning of life, especially of *your* life. Appreciate all that goes on around you. Do not deprecate anything. See magic and mystery and a challenge in the fact of your actual existence.

2 Make sure your bodily functions keep good pace with your health programme. Control your vitamin and mineral and protein intake without becoming paranoid about it. Good food makes for good thinking.

3 Discover whether or not you truly believe in Providence as an influence that tells you what to do and say at any given time. Find out whether you really believe in some power capable of dictating wise, positive moves on your part. Try to accept that help can be forthcoming in moments when the world seems to be falling around your feet, walls are closing in on you, no one likes you or wants to help you. In such negative moments it is of great help to feel that assistance can be forthcoming, if you help yourself as well.

4 Don't live in a fool's paradise. Face facts when they have to be faced. Get a firm sense of values and keep your inherent and ingrained standards of life. Don't try to change them to suit the requirements of others or their demands upon you. Use your mental and physical energies every day for constructive and creative works for yourself and for others. Let each hour of each day carry you forward successfully to an even more successful tomorrow.

5 Find a kind of joy in all that you do each day. Spread this joy and this optimism to others and you will get it back a hundredfold. You will see yourself mirrored in the eyes of others with whom you work and relax. When work ceases for the day do not take it home with you. Rest and unwind and turn your thinking processes to quite different outlets. That will prepare you well to meet the challenges of tomorrow.

6 Cultivate even more intelligence and intellect than you already possess by reading lively and informative newspapers and books. And get out and about if and when you can. Listen to people of intelligence and intellect and learn from them. Good music is well worth listening to as a harmonious contrast to conversation from time to time.

7 Try to be calm, cool and laid-back in all circumstances and conditions, more especially when crisis threatens. Nothing inspires calmness from others more than calmness from *you*. Train your nervous system not to jump at unexpected sounds or to get jangled when others lose their tempers around you.

8 Accept that you are *you* and that you have a definite responsibility to yourself to retain that priceless positive independence in the face of all opposition. At the end of it all you will be a well-liked, positive person.

23

SELL YOURSELF AS A POSITIVE COMMODITY

It seems quite reasonable to suggest that hardly a day goes by when we do not have to 'sell' an idea of some sort to another person or group of people. Even to ourselves.

Which leads to the cliché that all life is a question of salesmanship.

But, on reflection, it *is*, of course. And that is why the positive minded person makes the best and the most 'sales', which begin, quite naturally, in the act of selling oneself.

Personal salesmanship involves, not the gift of the gab, but energy and vitality and a knowledge of what our prospective 'customer' wants and expects from us.

Self-expression born of positive confidence in oneself and in what one wants and means to *get* is the keynote of successful self-selling. You may want to sell an idea to your bank manager for a loan, to your boss for a new scheme, or to a solicitor for assistance in a legal wrangle. If you can express yourself in simple, well-chosen, persuasive words that have a positive ring about them you will hold and keep the favourable attention of your opponent. Your words, expressions and explanations must be free from subterfuge, a truthful explanation of facts and figures. Such positive self-expression should lead your opponent to be *glad* to extend to you the service that you require, *pleased* to become involved with you.

If you have a proposition to put to someone, the acceptance of which will make you a happier person, controlled breathing is of the essence. Uncontrolled breathing makes it difficult to speak coherently and in measured tones. Naturally, this gives a bad impression to your listener. They note you are on 'panic stations' and are quite likely to take unfair advantage of this and to beat you down in your arguments. Control your breathing by taking a deep breath and exhaling slowly before beginning to press home your points. This applies to the simplest of sessions where you are wishing to impress somebody or ask someone for something important.

The word 'No' is always so ready to come to the lips of a person who is being asked for something by somebody. Saying 'No' prevents difficulties and possible complications and effort on the part of whoever is being confronted. Therefore the positive thinker will make it of paramount importance to 'sell' his proposition by quickly pointing out the benefits that will result from his plea being answered by the word 'Yes' rather than by 'No'. The positive thinker will temporarily dismiss his own possible benefits in favour of emphasizing his opponent's possible benefits, should his answer be in the affirmative. The quickness of the thought deceives the ear. And the mind also.

24

SPEAK POSITIVELY IN EVERYTHING YOU SAY

Following on the previous chapter concerned with selling yourself in a positive-minded manner, let us now take into consideration five most important facets of self-selling: voice, speech content, vocabulary, sincerity and planning.

Voice

Make it well-modulated. That is to say, do not speak in a sing-song voice, but with emphasis to show due consideration has been given to the words. End a sentence with an 'uplift' note in your voice rather than a downward note. Uplift is always positive, with promise of more interesting facts to come. Downwards suggests finality and a sudden end to the matter. Speaking is, after all, singing without the music in one's voice. But it must never develop into a monotonous monologue. There can be infinite 'music' put into the spoken word, a 'music' that gives colour and harmony and change of pace to words and phrases and expressions. Harmonious speech hypnotises, soothes and calms the listener as well as holding their attention and convincing them of your positive-mindedness. Paint 'mind-pictures' in all that you say.

Speech content

Always have something constructive to say when putting a proposition over. Cut a long story short to avoid confusion and boredom on the part of your listener. Articulate well and emphasize well the most vital and important parts of your proposition or argument. Refer back to the chapters on thought technology further back in this book and apply a genuine technique in the construction of your attempt to sell yourself as a positive person. Avoid all opening banalities such as the weather, current news items, family affairs and all such topics that are of no interest and which will bore the prospective purchaser of the positive ideas you wish to put over. No preambles or sketchy introductions to your main theme. Plunge in at once.

Vocabulary

Avoid trying to make an impression by the use of long, complicated words and phrases which you think will impress. Short, pithy words and phrases make a far better impression. Avoid the danger of using words you think are clever and sophisticated in an attempt to give the idea you are more worldly than probably you are. And certainly do not use slang words or expressions to suggest you are 'one of the lads (or girls)'.

Sincerity

When putting your positive proposition over do not gush or try to soft-soap your opponent with false compliments or flattery. This may please them but may not convince them of your sincerity. When you are taking part in an important meeting with the aim of getting what you want, by all means indicate to your opponent that you know they have the power to provide you with what you want. You need not, though, use extravagant words that, once again, will amount to flattery. Just ensure that they are in no doubt that you know what your objective is and that they can fulfil it. They will not wish to appear negative in the face of these positive projections of your faith and belief in them.

Planning

When embarking on an important meeting where you know you will need to impress someone, plan ahead several days before the vitial interview. Do not trust to luck or sudden inspirational ideas. They may not occur to you and you may well lose out through lack of forward planning. Whatever it is you wish to achieve, marshal your thoughts into a carefully prepared programme that will present your proposition in easy, but ever progressive, steps. There must be a logical beginning, middle and end that will embrace why you want such and such a thing, how you plan to get it and what you will do with it when you have it. Confused thinking on the spur of the moment will throw you off balance and baffle your listener. This personal planning programme can apply to an important job interview, to a meeting with your bank manager or with the head of your firm when promotion is desired; it can be brought into play when applying for membership of a coveted club you wish to join, even, in fact, to the very human situation of proposing marriage. After all, every situation is a battle of wits in which the better man or woman will surely win. The better person, being, of course, the positive-minded person.

No one in their right sense can ever deny that the entire world and the existence of every single civilised being in it is controlled by the amazing influence of the power of positive, outwardly-projected thought. Thought precedes words and these thoughts precipitate actions and actions produce results. And it is upon those results that the world relies.

POSITIVE THINKING THROUGH THE FORTIES

When men and women reach the age of 40 they are in the prime of life. That is not merely a cliché, it is a fact. Half a reasonable lifespan. However, today unemployment often sets in because of the current emphasis on youth as far as work is concerned. Men and women in their forties are often considered too old to be able to work in the present, progressive world of industry and computerisation. Redundancy rears its ugly head and some people in their fifties are given clocks and gold watches; smug testimonials referring to years of diligent work and service to the company are waved in front of their eyes. And all this in lieu of continued safe employment. Golden handshakes are deemed ample compensation for the prospect of empty years ahead, long before normal retirement is supposed to occur. Youth steps in and takes over and many a family is torn apart by living on benefit and scraping to preserve its self-respect.

This is the sort of bleak picture that faces many an executive or manager who thought they had a secure job until retirement. When redundancy threatens and they are still perhaps in their forties, it is difficult to remain positive about life. As the weeks go by and they receive rejection after rejection, it is all too easy to give up hope. Then the family suffers, friends stop calling as they no longer recognise the optimistic, forward-thinking person they once knew. Instead there is a person broken by circumstances, who feels they are no longer of any use to society and wonders how they are going to fill the years ahead and keep the family together, let alone provide them with the lifestyle they have been used to.

If their area of industry has decided it will go for the younger set, then there is no way they can hid their greying hair or the crow's-feet round the eyes. It was the case in former years that these outward signs showed experience and wisdom, so they must remember that *they* haven't changed – what has changed is the perception of society. Now companies feel that to appear vibrant, confident and revolutionary they must present a youthful face to competitors or to others they wish to do business with.

If, after exploring all the avenues of employment in their own sphere, they are still without a job, positive thinkers must realise that at 45, 50 or 55 they have still much to offer, not least of which is experience, not just of their profession, but of life in general and people. They must now apply themselves to finding a new outlet for their talents. It may take some searching, but one will surely exist. It may not, at first or even ever, provide the same standard of living as before but as long as it is an enjoyable job that they feel they can do well then their self-respect and the respect and admiration of family and friends is assured.

Positive thinkers will muse pleasantly on what life has done for them so far. Redundancy pay or savings or both will doubtless give them a breathing space to recover from the shock of losing their job. They will be free to review what they have done in life up to that point and will also be able to make plans for making life even more fulfilling in the future.

Look at your situation in this way. You have learned how to suffer and to be happy. You have probably lived through most crises from A to Z. Now you know so much. People have learnt to respect you in the past and you are not going to lose that respect now. Look out for tomorrow. Don't think back on the negative things of yesterday any more. Living in the past is regressive. Living in the present with hopes for the future is the only positive thing to do. Think of those whom you know who are possibly in worse trouble than you. Perhaps some of them are really suffering. The least of *your* troubles is that you are in your forties. Realise that you still have your eyesight. You can walk well on two firm feet. You can still hear well and speak well. And isn't your mind still as clear as a bell? You have a bed on which to sleep and a table at which to eat. How about now trying to utilise the things you have always known you are good at, but have never had the time in which to indulge them? Those long-forgotten hobbies. Those surprising talents and abilities you have never been able to explore and exploit. Maybe people will tell you it is time to ease up a little: 'You are not so young as you used to be'. Think of abounding good health now that your business brain is not going to be so overtaxed. Take a good look at yourself in the mirror. What's in a wrinkle or two? A few grey hairs? Lines on the forehead make you look learned. And so you should be at 40.

Youth may well set the pace these days but the middle-aged keep it going.

If you have children don't let them think that at 40 you are in your dotage. Let them realise it is the age when they can turn to you for advice, companionship, help in times of trouble. When you are 40 your children are probably at an age when they most need you.

Positive thinking may not get you another consistent job in life, but there is always an opportunity for a spare-time job of some sort in your local community, or where security guards are needed, or caretakers, or minicab drivers. Such jobs need people of maturity and a sense of responsibility. Never look down on such occupations as being beneath you, comparing them unfavourably with your past occupation, which may have been more demanding.

And a last word of advice for those over 40:

1 Think young and you will feel young.

2 If you disregard your age so will others.

3 Gentle exercise, taken regularly, will keep you mentally and physically alert.

4 It is your personality, not your age, that matters.

26

NEGATIVE ATTITUDES THAT DESTROY POSITIVE THINKING

Seven years is deemed to be the age of reason; 16 the age of consent and 18 the age of adulthood.

From 18 onwards men and women are victims of various negative attitudes towards life that tend to fog positive thinking and, in many cases, completely destroy it. They are the inadequates who become so accustomed to thinking in negative terms that they develop into defeatists and, in serious cases, into paranoiacs. To be paranoid is to suffer from a persecution complex that persuades you that everyone is against you. Very often it becomes far easier to be negative and to remain negative than to shake oneself free and to let positive thinking and positive attitudes take over. This is taking the line of least resistance. To many people this is, in fact, the easy answer to having to put up a fight against forbidding odds. Such individuals can be summed up as being immature, emotionally mixed up, insecure, unsure, lonely, fearing and accepting failure easily, searching for means to escape responsibility, easily led, incapable, inadequate, often self-centred, frustrated, repressed and inhibited.

Altogether an unfortunate mixed bag of negativism!

As far as health and mental attitude are concerned, these people can also be hypochondriacal, escapist, obstructionist, defeatist, pessimistic and victims to acute self-pity. In addition, they may also enjoy reliving past horrors and failures. To that add morbidity, a preoccupation with death; they may sometimes be suicidal, or suffer from neuroticism and obsession.

Religious faith, or the lack of it, can produce a confusing mixture of positive and negative attitudes in people. At different times they can experience the following conditions:

Negative	Positive
Lack of a spiritual sheet anchor	Spiritually secure
Overly religious fixation	Firm belief in their religion
Feelings of fatalism	Belief that a force for good is behind everything
Belief in nothing, so finds it difficult to achieve peace of mind	Intellectually uplifted
Occasional doubts	Belief that we are not able to understand everything
Lack of faith	Trust in faith
Anxiety state	Peace of mind

Without stressing the subject too strongly, so as not to confuse nor to antagonise those who do not follow any religious persuasion, a little faith really *does* go a long way! Having faith in *something*, whatever shape or form it may take, is a positive attitude in its own right. Some folk believe in God, or in spiritualism or incarnation or in life hereafter or in fate or Providence or, in fact, in any word or expression they may choose as a sheet anchor in life to assist in overcoming negative fear-thoughts, dread of death, dread of what is to happen to them after death. Such beliefs and hopes are healthy, positive and soul-saving. They stand for positivism as opposed to the negativism of the hopeless individual who feels there is nothing to hang on to in life and nothing to hope for after death.

If that is well and truly the case, why be given life only to have nothing in life and nothing after death? Why be born at all, in fact? Such thoughts and doubts spell insecurity. Insecurity gives rise to inadequacy and to be inadequate means one just cannot face up to life, much less to death. We are, here, concerned with life.

Decide, here and now – if you have not given it a thought before – that *you* have a sheet anchor in *your* life and as you allow the positive thought to look larger you will be able to turn to that invisible 'thing' or 'person' and know that 'it' will guide and help you through trouble, will help you banish all negative thinking and come shining through with positive thoughts for your present and for your future.

27

HOW POSITIVE THINKING CAN MAKE YOU POPULAR

Being popular in your social, business and domestic circles is probably what you most wish for in life, for being likeable is a personal commodity that can bring pleasant rewards.

Positive thinking may prompt you to speak your mind when dealing with others, by calling a spade a spade in no uncertain terms when forced to do so. In short, that sort of positive-mindedness does not beat about the bush, nor indulge in soft-soaping others. Straight talk is the order of the day and this very often commands considerable respect. However, tact and restraint are vitally necessary in situations that have to be handled with delicacy. It is the person who gets things in perspective who fully appreciates this and does not permit honest confrontations to get out of hand. In other words, always bring tact and diplomacy into play.

When we know we are well-liked by those around us we begin to like ourselves as well, which is another way of feeling adequate.

One fail-safe way of being liked is to like others and to demonstrate that fact in as many positive ways as possible. They will see themselves mirrored in *you* and will try to model themselves on you. If the mirrored image is good, *they* will become good.

If you want others to like and to appreciate and to accept you in all your walks in life, you will most certainly avoid:

insulting them;

attempting to boss them;

obviously trying to correct them;

consistently nagging them;

trying to show how superior you are;

belittling them in any way;

making them feel inadequate (even if you know they are)!

Positive-mindedness prompts co-operation with others rather than opposition. Even if it annoys and frustrates you for a while. Even if and when you know them to be in the wrong. Positive thought prompts patience in the long run, and patience invariably pays off.

Another aspect of positivity making you likeable to others lies in the following commendable restraints:

not making yourself aloof and 'mysterious';

not showing off or 'playing to the gallery';

not preaching at others.

People like to be told that you, in fact, have been in a similar situation when they explain to you a mistake *they* have made. It makes them feel less alone in their errors, makes you a confidant(e), more especially if you tell them what you did in order to rectify your mistake.

Most certainly the positive thinker *thinks* before they get aggressive with anyone. Holding back when the gall rises is good. Force often frightens – if only force with words.

There are lots of shy folk around, everywhere. They need to be put at their ease. Who better to do this than the positive thinker, *you*, for instance?

We have already mentioned the loner and the eccentric. Another type of negative-minded character is the recluse, the solitary. Yet another is the intellectual hermit who takes refuge from society in their intellectualism that they imagine raises them above all others. Such people are not exactly popular and, in any case, such characters are really inadequates in their own right. So don't let being positive-minded give you the impression it puts you above others on those exaggerated planes of thought.

Loners are not generally liked. Nor understood.

Likeability from a positive point of view also embraces the ability to make it easy for others to meet you, to greet you, to talk to you, to confide in you. Good manners follow upon consideration for others, because positive thought is involved in the way in which you socialise and in the way you mix with business partners. Even in the domestic circle good manners are appreciated rather than a 'letting-your-hair-down' attitude because you are at home. People do care what you do, or say or look like, even in the familiar surroundings of your own home.

A little positive thought will show you how others will like you to share their hobbies, interests, abilities and capabilities, hopes and dreams. If advice can be given, give it. If not, be interested in their misgivings and try to share them.

When others *do* approach you for advice take time to listen. The mere fact of listening will make them like you. Good listeners are sometimes appreciated far more than good talkers, who often have a tendency to talk about themselves rather than the other person.

Positive, personally-projected thought, as observed elsewhere in this book, reaches the readily receptive minds of those with whom you come into contact and friends are made in double-quick time. It would be gratifying for you to know that you are thought of as a 'tower of strength'. Positive words and advice can create that without recourse to cash or any material assistance. Positive words can inspire. Negative words can destroy. As, perhaps, others have tried to destroy *you* in the past, with their negative approaches to your problems.

So now you know the score!

1 Personal positivity is the shining aura that surrounds an individual.

2 Positivity is a shimmering vibration that emanates from an individual.

3 Positivity is the colour of life, its brilliance, its harmony, its very breath.

4 Positivity is the appreciation of the power of personal thought as it affects you and as it affects others around you.

5 Positivity is the life-force from which springs the very essence of kindness and care for others who, in return, will care for *you*.

6 Positivity heightens insight and understanding by creating the capacity for understanding others.

And all those acceptable qualities radiate from the mind, which refuses all negative thinking despite all that may have happened in the past to attempt to destroy positive thinking and positive attitudes.

Mull those thoughts over in your mind, count your friends, your *real* friends, on as many fingers and thumbs as your two hands will accommodate, and see how you rate in *your* likeability chart!

28

DAILY DYNAMICS TO BOOST POSITIVE THINKING

Whatever you do during the week, a slight contrast in your behaviour pattern will give the positive and the negative sides of your nature a change to express themselves for the betterment of both.

We have suggested in a previous chapter that you cannot be positive all of the time. Relaxing a strict regime of positive thinking every so often gives the positive drive an opportunity to refresh and to renew itself so that, when conditions and circumstances call for direct thinking, the brain has been relaxed and the mind is once again ready to tackle problems in a forthright fashion.

Just as a fitness regime is good for the body, so a fitness regime can be good for the mind. Just as a fitness programme can include complete relaxation of the body one day and a strict session of exercise the next day to tone up the muscles, send the blood freshly circulating round the body and give added strength and elasticity to the muscles, so can complete relaxation of mental and emotional effort for one or two days a week tone up your thinking machine to make you doubly powerful, positive and effective on all the other days.

To that end, consider now the following programme of Daily Dynamics to be carried out on a weekly basis, probably varying the attitudes and actions for each day as the weeks go by so as to introduce variety into the programme and to prevent any staleness or routine or boredom from creeping in. The basic idea is to relax positive, concentrated effort one day and on the next day to go all out for renewed positive effort to win through and to overcome all obstacles. The days on which you relax and the days on which you use dynamic effort must be sensibly synchronised so that you apply the right thinking to the right day. If tomorrow is a day on which you know you are to be faced with overcoming a certain problem then that day is your day of real positive effort. Similarly, when you have an easy day coming up make that your day of relaxation in which you may pleasantly, and with a smile, give way to negative thoughts you know full well you will never really act upon.

Daily Dynamics for one week

To be repeated and varied as the weeks go by

Monday

Have a positive outlook from the moment you get up. This is to be a go-getter day! This is to be your day for being the 'I am' personality. Storm your way through the long hours of business, creativity, productivity. Project powerful positive thought to everyone around you. Say what you think and consider carefully everything you say. Dash all negative opposition by positive action.

Tuesday

Today try being a yes-man or woman. Find amusement in the reactions of those around you who are ready to be opposed by you in your 'strong man' role. See what it feels like to say 'Yes' to everyone with whom you work. You will stagger and perplex them. Flop out mentally and let others take responsibility for a brief period. Give your mind a rest from positive mental effort. It will be hard at first, but it will put others doubly on their guard, for they will just not comprehend the apparent sudden change in your tactics.

Wednesday

Get up early. Do deep breathing exercises before an open window. Fill your mind with positive thoughts. At work or at business (or whatever will occupy you for this day) once again launch into your positive-mindedness, letting no opposition get the better of you. Benefit now from the negative attitudes of yesterday that no doubt took your colleagues by surprise. Reassert yourself with a refreshed mind and an even more powerful projection of positive thought. Relax in the evening with satisfaction at a good day's work done, your confidence in yourself restored and your companions once again baffled.

Thursday

Today, decide not to be perhaps quite so positive minded, but not so negative as you were on Tuesday. Keep your workmates or office acquaintances guessing as to your attitudes. Be quiet and restrained in everything that you do and say. Offer the velvet glove with a hint of iron fingers.

Friday

Now, this is another positive day for you. Assert yourself a before. Project those powerful thought projections of yours that you now know to be so effective. Yesterday you relaxed a great deal, but not totally. Today you feel strengthened in mind and in body, so go to it once more.

Saturday

Today is your day of relaxation provided your schedule does not include working on a Saturday. If you *are* free of work, or even if you are not, allow this day to be a day of positive-negative thought! A day in which you can weigh the pros and cons of your existence, your work life, your social life, your domestic life. A day of searching self-analysis in which you decide if what you are doing is right for you and what is going the wrong way for you. Count up your week's successes when you have been positive minded and remember what happened when you decided to be negative for a change. Review your gains and your losses on those separate occasions. Realise then, how the positive phases were far more successful than the negative ones, but recall, also, that there were a few lessons you learned *from* being negative for a while.

Sunday

Today plan with vision and with a thought for the immediate future. Relax your mind from its positive attitude and take things easy. Nevertheless, think well about the week to come, merely a few hours away. Decide the changes you are going to make in the forthcoming Daily Dynamics programme. Choose the days for being positive and decide on which days you are going to be negative. Review your past week's positive successes and negative failures.

Repeat this Daily Dynamics routine for say, either four weeks or just one week in every month. But *do* it. Knowing you are deliberately going to give yourself a rest from powerful positive thinking from time to time will do your mind a world of good. There comes a time when the brain needs a short rest from positive effort. If, by now, you have *really* developed the power of positive thinking – and if you now realise that positive thought *is* the greatest factor for happy living and ultimate success in life – you will have also accepted that the most dynamic of minds needs its programmed resting periods. The Daily Dynamics routine, as explained, will doubtless do that for *your* mind.

29

NOW SUMMARISE ALL YOU HAVE LEARNT ABOUT POSITIVE THOUGHT

The revelation of the power of positive thought will probably have opened your eyes somewhat and will, hopefully, have helped you to realise that life *can* be even more fulfilling for you in the future if you follow the precepts and the maxims laid down.

In order to assist you to revise all you have learnt about the amazing influence of positive thinking and to suggest various chapters that may have been of special and immediate value to you in your particular search for personal happiness and success in your life, here is a summary of all that has been explained.

1 You have realised that negative thoughts from the past have very definitely and very often a damaging effect on your present moves, capable of destroying your hopes for the future. These negative thoughts and impressions and memories have ranged from your childhood days with your parents, your experiences in your school-days, things of an adverse nature that may have happened to you in your early working days, emotional mistakes made in connection with your first love-relationship, through to the many and varied past experiences in your young and growing adulthood.

2 These negative past memories and impressions have been countered and overcome by suggestions for positive thoughts for the present, with a heavy and important bearing on your future.

3 You have considered the possibility of being an 'I am' personality. You have realised the importance of being an 'I am' personality from time to time in order to make positive thought work *for* you rather than *against* you.

4 The chapter on 'The career syndrome' has probably opened your eyes to the various emotional problems connected with starting a job, wanting a change of job, gaining a desired promotion, and the negative effects on you of losing your job or not having a job at all.

5 Following on that exploration of the career syndrome you have learnt about thought technology, no doubt an entirely new concept to you but, nevertheless, a concept that sums up the technology of positive and negative thought in the most simple of terms. Probably you have never regarded the thinking-process as an 'ology' apart from the much used and often abused application of personal psychology. Don't easily lose sight of this valuable 'new' science of the mind and its various emotions and its subtle division into positive and negative thinking.

6 After those interesting and revealing facts you have learnt that it is most important to specialise rather than to generalise. In short, to know a lot about something in particular rather than a lot about anything in general. You have also gathered that it is useful, if not imperative, that specialising in one special talent or ability in a positive manner is best exploited if your personality is seen to be compatible with that particular talent or specialised ability, in order that one is not at variance with the other.

7 Further, you have now accepted that the power of positive thought can give added strength to your body, to your physical well-being. It has been well demonstrated that, when the power of positive thought is forced into your arms, your hands, your body and your legs, the strength is doubled in intensity, so that you are pushing and pulling, not only with your body and with your limbs, but with your *mind* also. A one-hundred-per-cent effort is therefore turned into a two-hundred-per-cent effort.

8 Emotions, states of mind, hysteria and various expressions of horror, pleasure, fright, joy and sadness have been explained by describing your brain as the thinking machine that, of course, it so patently *is*. You have learnt how to manipulate and to control that complex machine in its influences over your mind and your body.

9 After those revelations, the domestic scene has come in for analysis and the application of positive thought as applied to the family and the happy and the successful upbringing of children. You will have realised that positive thought should, by no means, be abandoned in the safety and the sanctity of the family circle. That, in fact, its application is just as vital in that sphere as it is in business and in the social scene.

10 Thought technology has been taken several steps further in the chapter following that about the domestic scene in order that you should not lose sight of its impact upon your various attitudes to life and the serious effects mismanagement of mind can have upon you in terms of depression and defeatism.

11 Vision and creativity, visualisation and realisation according to the power of positive thinking have followed, in which you have found that suddenly discovering a fresh outlet in life can lead to exciting new events. You have seen that if you see, feel, want, desire and attract something very special and very dear to you, you *can* get it.

12 After that, your attention has been turned to the vital subject of stress – something you will surely have experienced from time to time so far in your life. You have seen the difference between stressful thinking and hopeful thinking and how stress can be dissolved by positive thought, rest and relaxation, in order to avoid having a nervous breakdown, which is nature's way of telling you you have had enough for a while.

13 The tremendous power of positive thought projection has been revealed, expressed, not only in the way you project your thoughts, but in the question of your personal appearance being consistent *with* your positive thought projections. The question of making a vital impression upon others has been stressed. The question of an opponent's counter-positive thought projections against you in a battle of wits has been revealed. The subtle mechanics of projecting positive thought to others in order to win through and to get what is most desired has been amply demonstrated in the ability to 'will' your thoughts into the mind of your opponent in such a powerful manner as to force them to be received by him or her and acted upon.

14 Here it was suggested that you cannot be positive all of the time. The brain and the mind need a rest as does the body and you have been well advised not to overdo things. Refreshed by some relaxation from positive thinking you have seen how you can return to the fray with renewed determination and power.

15 Tense situations, causing tension as well as stress, have been demonstrated in a few very simple, day-to-day situations such as a visit to the dentist, the fear of awaiting an operation, the trauma of taking a driving test and having to address an audience – just a few examples of situations that can be equalled to any dreaded event in which you may be involved. Ways of dismissing tension of that sort and many others have, hopefully, relaxed you already.

16 The question of personal philosophy has been raised in relation to personal thought power. Direct and obvious links between thought, attitudes and a firm philosophy have been revealed.

17 The Americans are fond of telling us to 'Have a good day!' You have gone through your 'Formula for having a good day' and have probably found it most useful. There are so many good things you *can* do to make each day really good and constructive. Now you know them all. Also, you have read the 'Table of reverse attitudes' that could possibly make your day a very, very bad day indeed.

18 Following on these cases illustrating the negative evils of nervous tension, you will have appreciated the great value of meaning something to someone in life, a really great creator of positive thought for, when you mean something to someone, that someone also means a great deal to you and the menace of negative thinking is dealt a severe blow. In such pleasant and often loving situations, extroversion is the dominant theme and introversion just cannot get a look in.

19 A strong character in terms of the ability to cultivate positive thinking is well stressed as a follow-up, and an analysis of good and bad character traits makes it abundantly clear how negative thinking can destroy character whereas positive thought considerably enhances it.

20 Your positive-thinking characteristics are well revealed in a personal quiz which delves quite intimately into things you do and things you think about yourself and about others. Probably you have, by now, identified with many of the questions to your delight or to your dismay. In any case, you no longer undervalue nor underestimate yourself.

21 You have studied the eight ways to make yourself a positive person. You have no doubt found them to be extremely simple and easy to follow and easy to live up to. There is really nothing at all complicated about being a positive person. Millions are, after all. It's just a question of knowing how.

22 The chapter on selling yourself as a positive commodity may have amused, but you will have seen a deal of wisdom in it, for, after all, life *is* a continual process of self-selling.

23 The question of a positive purpose in life is simply and graphically explained in the way in which you speak and express yourself and your positive thoughts behind all that you have to say. Speech impresses a tremendous amount and voice control is of the essence, as you will have now realised.

24 Getting near to the end of this book you have read about the fear of the forties that these days unfortunately afflicts so many men and women, especially where employment is concerned. In your case, whatever your age, you will have found encouragement in the in-depth analysis of those prime years in the lifetime of men and women. It is to be hoped that that period of life will not any longer hold any fears for you.

25 Following that, you have delved into an analysis of negative attitudes that destroy positive thinking. They may possibly have surprised you by their destructive content, but it's far better knowing the worst than living in a fool's paradise and continuing to think in a negative manner.

26 You have appreciated how positive thinking can make you popular with others. And who doesn't want to be well-liked? Most certainly we all do.

27 And now you will have made a note of your Daily Dynamics to boost positive thinking.   So go to it!

CONCLUSION

And indeed, what *do* we conclude?

That if you have not already got there, there is still plenty of time *to* get there because now you realise the potential of your brain power, the mechanics of your mind and the application of thought technology in the pursuit and the development of the power of positive thought.

Things that, yesterday, may have seemed impossible to accomplish are now seen to be well within the range and the scope of your personal attainment.

You have learnt how to exercise control over your subconscious mind that brings up past, negative impressions and memories and to replace these negative memories with conscious thoughts for the present and for the future.

You know now that without conscious control of past painful memories your subconscious mind would impose upon you what it chooses and your conscious thoughts would become uncontrolled. Thoughts and actions would be undisciplined and you would become victim to many perplexities.

The mind can be a masquerader. It can realistically imitate diseases of the mind and the body if permitted to do so. Positive thought can and does baffle this offshoot of negative thinking and can dismiss psychosomatic symptoms of ill-health and discontent.

As far as you, personally, are concerned, the simple knowledge of the mechanics of your mind and the ease with which you can develop and cultivate positive thinking is now in your possession for all time. There should be no going back.

Further interesting and helpful titles from FOULSHAM.

THE POWER OF SELF-HYPNOSIS
The Key to Confidence
By Gilbert Oakley
ISBN: 0-572-01135-0

A valuable self-help course from a well known author who helps the reader to understand the reasons for problems that undermine self-confidence, and to deal with them effectively.

DEVELOP YOUR IQ
By Gilles Azzopardi
ISBN: 0-572-01934-3

Everyone can benefit from the IQ-style tests that are carefully geared to the four basic criteria of intelligence: numerical calculation, spatial perception, verbalisation, reason and logic.

CHECK YOUR IQ
By Ken Russell & Philip Carter
ISBN: 0-572-01807-X

Featuring 400 IQ questions, arranged in a series of quizzes and exercises you can see how your IQ measures up. You can treat the questions like an exam, or just enjoy testing your own brain power.

MEASURE YOUR IQ
By Gilles Azzopardi
ISBN: 0-572-01935-1

Structured puzzles, diagrams and word-teasers of the kind used to assess doctors and teachers, offer a reliable guide to your intellectual grading. Away from the pressures of the exam room, these questions are not only intriguing but fun too!

SUCCEED AT IQ TESTS
By Gilles Azzopardi
ISBN: 0-572-01948-3

Study the workings of the famous IQ tests, spot your own strengths and weaknesses and improve – fast. Your IQ may be higher than you think.

STRENGTHEN YOUR PERFORMANCE IN PSYCHOLOGICAL TESTS
By Cecile Cesari
ISBN: 0-572-02208-5

Psychological tests are a major factor in today's employment selection process. Anyone can learn how to handle these questions more successfully.

TRAIN YOUR BRAIN FOR A FAST-TRACK CAREER
By Dr Jacqueline Renaud
ISBN: 0-572-02290-5

Dr Renaud describes her book as a box of tools for the brain. Use the exercises and puzzles to tune yourself to turbo performance!

50 BEST MEMORY METHODS AND TESTS
By Michael Dansel
ISBN: 0-572-02282-4

Everyone knows the frustration of racking your brains to remember something. But this annoying everyday occurrence can be overcome. Your memory is like a muscle. It can be trained to produce amazing results – which get you noticed.

STRENGTHEN YOUR MEMORY
A Self Improvement Course
By Michael Fidlow
ISBN: 0-572-01609-3

This book could change your life! You will learn to remember people, their names, jokes, stories, spelling, things to do. Sounds marvellous, doesn't it. Well it is – and it could very well be you.

THE SPEED TECHNIQUE TO ALPHA MEDITATION AND VISUALISATION
By Harold Kampf
ISBN: 0-572-02155-0

In this book, Harold Kampf has achieved a breakthrough. He has developed an accelerated technique which is easy to apply and produces results in meditation or visualisation.

PLAN YOUR PERSONAL INSURANCE LIKE AN EXPERT
By Philip Raine
ISBN: 0-572-02190-9

By an experienced insurance broker this book will tell you what to buy and why and lead you through the jargon of insurance claim forms.

PLAN YOUR INVESTMENTS LIKE AN EXPERT
By Steven Berry
ISBN: 0-572-02215-8

The world of investments is too often seen as daunting and mysterious. But if you have the right strategy, it can be so easy to make money. Steven Berry, as successful financial adviser introduces you to the experts' secrets.

THE COMPLETE PROFESSIONAL HORSE RACING SYSTEM
By W J Davies
ISBN: 0-572-01713-8

A ready-to-win betting system which will show you how to back the odds and bet more like a Bookmaker than a punter, and win like a Bookmaker!